THE TIRELESS TRAVELER

In every work regard the writer's end;
None e'er can compass more than they intend.

—POPE

THE
TIRELESS
TRAVELER

Twenty Letters to the Liverpool Mercury by

ANTHONY TROLLOPE

1875

Edited, with an Introduction, by

BRADFORD ALLEN BOOTH

UNIVERSITY OF CALIFORNIA PRESS

BERKELEY, LOS ANGELES, LONDON

University of California Press
Berkeley, California

University of California Press, Ltd.
London, England

First Paperback Printing 1978
ISBN: 0-520-03723-5

Printed in the United States of America

1 2 3 4 5 6 7 8 9 0

TO
HYDER EDWARD ROLLINS

ACKNOWLEDGMENTS

To PRESIDENT ROBERT GORDON SPROUL of the University of California and to the faculty advisory committee on research I owe sincere thanks for the grant that enabled me to trace these articles. I am also indebted to the officials of the Henry E. Huntington Library for permission to reprint several paragraphs from my article in *The Huntington Library Quarterly*, "Trollope in California," and to the Harvard College Library for photostatic transcripts. It is a pleasure to add a word of appreciation to my colleague, Edward Niles Hooker, for suggestions, and to Mr. John Floyd and Mr. William Leary for invaluable assistance.

B.A.B.

CONTENTS

CONTENTS—*Continued*

CONTENTS—*Continued*

CONTENTS — Continued

INTRODUCTION

IT IS WITH no thought of adding to Anthony Trollope's stature as a writer that I present these long-lost articles. Prosaically factual, many of them do not have his customary grace of style and warmth of manner. Yet they are important.

For Trollope's biographers these articles fill out the pattern of an eight months' trip to Australia about which virtually nothing was known. For the social historian they preserve faithfully and in minutest detail a picture of Ceylon and Australia in transition. For the economist they describe, in a concrete manner that is denied mere statistical surveys, under what circumstances of poverty and prosperity British colonists actually lived. For all lovers of literature they add a not insignificant book to the bibliography of Anthony Trollope, and thus must concern that widening stream of readers who are reaffirming the old novelist's many virtues.

The casual reader, glancing over Trollope's bibliography, probably overlooks the twelve titles of biography, essays, and travels, for the world has refused to accept Trollope's extravagant estimate of these books, and rightly chooses to remember him as a novelist. But to understand completely a man's nature one must take cognizance of his less felicitous works. Trollope was a creative artist, but he did not live in a dream world of fantasy. He was a practical man of affairs.

Writing was to him a vocation, and he pursued it methodically. The little band of aesthetes who contended that the divine afflatus alone produces a work of art howled execrations against him from the safety of their pale magazines. They said he was a beef-fed Philistine. Common citizens, accustomed to thinking of literary men in terms of Oscar Wilde's red velveteen breeches, were confused. Here was a writer whose habits were no more eccentric than their own, whose three passions—hunting, traveling, and work—were as commonplace as suet pudding. Whoso would be a literary man must be a nonconformist. Trollope was obviously an impostor. He was too normal in his enthusiasms and too ready in his acceptance of conventions to be a significant writer. But it was somehow comforting to remember that old Trollope was on the job, batting out common-sense novels with the regularity and precision with which his postal carriers delivered the morning mail. It was reassuring to be reminded with each new book that Dover's cliffs, though crumbling around the edges, were still white. It was pleasant to hear him banging around the world, full of British optimism and looking surprisingly like John Bull himself. One could count on Trollope's knowing the value of a sack of potatoes or a hogshead of wine in every port in the world.

The elements of Trollope's practical nature are nowhere better illustrated than in his travel books and letters. Here one meets a man very different from the sedate chronicler of drowsy Barsetshire. Trollope on tour must have been an awesome sight, plowing like a battle-tank ponderously but relentlessly over frontier obstructions, inconveniences, and hardships. With the doggedness of the professional researcher he pursued the tangible and the intangible constituents of a foreign culture, putting poet and peasant, as well as commerce and industry, under glass for the satisfaction of his insatiable curiosity. He was a statistical Baedeker bulling his way over a strange terrain, notebook in hand, with one eye cocked, businesslike, on the economic condition of the people, while the other, that of the novelist, detected their individual and collective foibles. But most of his observations of men and manners were reserved for the novels; the travel books are encyclopedias of practical information, with particular advice on how to wangle a decent living out of a struggling colony.

Writers ordinarily travel either to amuse themselves while storing up armaments for another assault upon Parnassus, or to search for new inspiration in exotic scenes and peoples. Not so Trollope. He traveled either officially in the line of his occupational duties as postal missioner, or unofficially as self-appointed guardian of colonial welfare. He traveled no royal road of romance to delight jaded clubwomen, nor did he immortalize his impressions in a series of frothy essays. Trollope's interest was, as he says, "the political, social, and material condition of these countries."[1] Much has been made of the fact that his few comments on art, architecture, and landscape are so stereotyped. Unlike professional aesthetes, he was too conventional to hunt for beauty where it had never been found, and too

[1] Anthony Trollope, *An Autobiography*, 2 vols., Edinburgh, 1883, II, 202.

honest to deny its presence where it was universally acknowledged. He *was* in many ways a tabloid tourist, an Innocent Abroad, his own "Tourist in Search of Knowledge," who is "no great frequenter of galleries, preferring the useful to the ornamental in his inquiries."[2] But it is only fair to remember his purpose, which was not to sing the glories of nature and man's imitations thereof, but to describe society. Like Dickens, Trollope was interested chiefly in men and women; like Browning, he loved nature, but human nature more. Nature to him was simply the setting against which men and women act.

Perhaps Trollope's purpose is best described in his own words. In the introductory chapter to *Australia and New Zealand* he cautions against passing snap judgment on young colonies,

the success of which must still in a great degree depend on the opinion respecting their condition which shall gradually spread itself among the inhabitants of the old world. Nothing that any of us can say or write can now influence much the prosperity of the United States. But there are still many in England who have to learn whether Australia is becoming a fitting home for them and their children, and the well-being of Australia still depends in a great degree on the tidings which may reach them. The great object of those

[2] *Travelling Sketches*, London, 1886, p. 78. Trollope continues (pp. 79–80): "He will listen with wondrous patience to the details of guides, jotting down figures in a little book, and asking wonder-working questions which no guide can answer. And he looks into municipal matters wherever he goes, learning all details as to mayors, aldermen, and councillors, as to custom duties on provisions, as to import duties on manufactures, as to schools, convents, and gaols, to scholars, mendicants, and criminals. He does not often care much for scenery, but he will be careful to inquire how many passengers the steamboats carry on the lakes, and what average of souls is boarded and lodged at each large hotel that he passes."

who undertake to teach any such lessons, should, I think, be to make the student understand what he, in his condition of life, may be justified in expecting there,—of what are the manner and form of life into which he may probably fall. With this object in view, hoping that by diligence I might be able to do something towards creating a clearer knowledge of these colonies, I have visited them all. Of each of them I have given some short account, and have endeavoured to describe the advancing or decreasing prosperity of their various interests. I hope I have done this without prejudice.[3]

This declaration applies to *all* his travel books, as well as to the newspaper articles which are here reprinted for the first time. Michael Sadleir[4] has tried to show that Trollope afterward in his novels made effective use of his travel experiences, but the evidence is not very convincing. Nearly two years in Australia produced only the novelette *Harry Heathcote of Gangoil* and some scenes for *John Caldigate*.

Trollope inherited his passion for travel honestly. Among the many well-known literary travelers of the nineteenth century who made themselves famous in England, notorious in America, was his mother. The popularity of Frances Trollope's *Domestic Manners of the Americans* (1832), an acidulous book inspired by the good lady's sundry misfortunes in the frontier city of Cincinnati, did much to make traditional the patronizing air with which British cosmopolites dismissed their unpolished American cousins. Her name became

---

[3] Anthony Trollope, *Australia and New Zealand*, 2 vols., London, 1873, I, 20–21.

[4] *Anthony Trollope: A Commentary*, London: Constable, 1927, pp. 176–178.

synonymous with globe-trotting, and was used by at least one writer as a common noun to denote the indefatigable tourist.[5] To say that Anthony followed in her footsteps is not to use a mere figure of speech.

Trollope's first travel book he considered his best. Moreover, in his autobiography he expressed the curious opinion that it was the best book he ever wrote.[6] *The West Indies and the Spanish Main* (1859) is good, but not so good as he believed. It is, indeed, "amusing, useful, and true"[7]—Trollope's criteria of excellence in a travel book; but Trollope lacked the artistic insight and the delicate fancy to raise it from the ruck of the ephemeral. It is distinguished from the other travel volumes, however, as Trollope realized,[8] by being eminently readable. Statistics are neglected in favor of personalities and amusing anecdote, and the tone is further lightened by the spontaneity of the comment. Of his unstudied effects Trollope was proud.

I never made a single note while writing or preparing it. Preparation, indeed, there was none. The descriptions and opinions came hot on to the paper from their causes. I will not say that this is the best way of writing a book intended to give accurate information. But it is the best way of producing to the eye of the reader, and to his ear, that which the eye of the writer has seen and his ear heard. There are two kinds of confidence which a reader may have in his author,—which two kinds the reader who wishes to use his reading well should carefully discriminate. There is a confidence in facts and a confidence in vision. The one man tells you accurately what has been. The other suggests to you

---

[5] *Anthony Trollope: A Commentary*, p. 89.
[6] *An Autobiography*, I, 172.
[7] *Ibid.*, I, 172.
[8] *Ibid.*, I, 218–221; II, 202.

what may, or perhaps what must have been, or what ought to have been. The former requires simple faith. The latter calls upon you to judge for yourself, and form your own conclusions. The former does not intend to be prescient, nor the latter accurate. Research is the weapon used by the former; observation by the latter. Either may be false,—wilfully false; as also may either be steadfastly true. As to that, the reader must judge for himself. But the man who writes *currente calamo*, who works with a rapidity which will not admit of accuracy, may be as true, and in one sense as trustworthy, as he who bases every word upon a rock of facts. I have written very much as I have travelled about; and though I have been very inaccurate, I have always written the exact truth as I saw it;—and I have, I think, drawn my pictures correctly.[9]

Distressed by the widespread effect of his mother's shortsighted view of America, Trollope devoted the second of his five trips to the United States to the accumulation of materials for a social and economic study that he hoped could correct the current misconceptions. The resulting volumes, *North America* (1862), are a hastily compiled, generally inaccurate *omnium-gatherum* of which he was afterward ashamed, but which has the virtue of a sympathetic approach arising from scrupulous disregard of British prejudices. *The Domestic Manners of the Americans*, he felt,[10] was a woman's book—tracing with a light pen American social defects and backwoods absurdities. *North America*, on the contrary, was to be a man's work, tracing with scholarly pen sociological causes and

[9] *An Autobiography*, I, 173–174.   [10] *North America*, I, 2.

effects. But it is neither accurate nor very interesting. With his customary honesty Trollope admitted its tedium and confusion: "I can recommend no one to read it now in order that he may be either instructed or amused."[11]

There is further evidence of the serious view which Trollope took of hasty and biased British generalizations on America. In the introductory chapter to his next travels, *Australia and New Zealand*, he writes:

An Englishman visiting the United States, if he have any purpose of criticism in his mind,—any intention of judging how far the manner of life there is a good manner, and of making comparison between British and American habits, should be ever guarding himself against the natural habit of looking at things only from his own point of view. . . . Should he find Americans to be educated, plenteously provided, honest, moral, and Godfearing, he might perhaps, in such case, safely conclude that they were prosperous and happy, even if they talked through their noses and called him Sir at every turn in their speech. . . . Such things may influence the happiness of an individual, may make the United States an uncomfortable home for a middle-aged Englishman, or London a dreary domicile for an American well established in his own customs. They have no bearing at all on the well being of a people, and yet they have often been taken as indicating a national deformity, and sometimes national calamity. Our writers have fallen into this mistake in writing of America.[12]

The volumes of *Australia and New Zealand* constitute Trollope's most ambitious colonial study, and rep-

---

[11] *An Autobiography*, I, 221.   [12] *Australia and New Zealand*, I, 19–21.

resent more time and painstaking effort than he put into any three novels. Yet the result is not satisfactory. Perhaps he grew weary of his subject. He had contracted to write at the same time a series of articles for the London *Daily Telegraph*.[13] The double task he set himself was too enervating to complete with unflagging spirit, and Pegasus sometimes loiters along like Ludlam's dog. The tedium of dead pages of facts and figures is too often unrelieved by the vitalizing force of dramatic presentation. Trollope is again the best critic of his own work:

It was a better book than that which I had written eleven years before on the American States, but not so good as that on the West Indies in 1859. As regards the information given, there was much more to be said about Australia than the West Indies. Very much more is said—and very much more may be learned from the latter than from the former book. I am sure that any one who will take the trouble to read the book on Australia, will learn much from it. But the West Indian volume was readable. I am not sure that either of the other works are, in the proper sense of that word. When I go back to them I find that the pages drag with me; —and if so with me, how must it be with others who have none of that love which a father feels even for his ill-favoured offspring. Of all the needs a book has the chief need is that it be readable. . . . But with all these faults the book was a thoroughly honest book, and was the result of unflagging labour for a period of fifteen months. I spared myself no trouble in inquiry, no trouble in seeing, and no trouble in listening. I throughly imbued my mind with the subject,

[13] For an account of this series see Bradford A. Booth, "Trollope in California," *The Huntington Library Quarterly*, III (October, 1939), 118.

and wrote with the simple intention of giving trustworthy information on the state of the Colonies.[14]

Until the discovery of the travel letters which make up this book, nothing was known of Trollope's second visit to Australia (1875) except the simple facts of his departure from London and his return. It has been assumed by his biographers that he sailed from Sydney directly to England. The last two articles of this series, however, describe his journey via Hawaii, San Francisco, and overland to New York. San Francisco newspapers record his arrival on the *City of Melbourne*, September 26, 1875, after a voyage of twenty-eight days.[15] He registered immediately at the Grand Hotel. The *Morning Call* was sufficiently aware of the city's distinguished visitor to have quoted from one of his stories on the day before his arrival, but to the *Chronicle* he was simply "A. Moltrope" [*sic*]![16]

Less than two years after his return to London the peripatetic novelist was off again, this time to South Africa. His experiences and observations were once more embalmed in two ponderous volumes, the contents of which will not hold children from play and old men from the chimney corner. One would think Trollope might have had his fill of wandering; but no, he was soon on a yacht bound for Iceland. On this occasion, freed from any moral duty to report the conclusions of a sober survey, he dashed off a genial *jeu*

---

[14] *An Autobiography*, II, 202–203.
[15] Notices of his arrival were carried in the *Evening Bulletin*, the *Morning Call*, the *Alta California*, and the *Chronicle*. See the issues of these papers for September 27, 1875.
[16] San Francisco *Chronicle*, September 27, 1875.

d'esprit which makes one wish he had more often subordinated information to informality. Certainly the present series of letters inspires that wish, for though they are not so factual as his published volumes on Australia, yet the method and manner are pretty much the same.

It should be remembered that Trollope was not the only literary man to visit and describe Australia. Richard Henry Horne, the friend of Elizabeth Barrett Browning, had published his *Australian Facts and Prospects*, as well as his *Australian Autobiography*, in 1859. Sampson Low's *Index to the British Catalogue of Books 1837–1857* lists 121 entries under Australia, as well as others under the several geographical subdivisions! Each succeeding year saw the appearance of many other surveys, in which every possible aspect of Australian life was examined.Trollope's information, then, cannot have been startlingly new. And since he had so recently told the story of Australia and passed elaborate judgment on its possibilities, what excuse was there for another account? This time he wrote for a newspaper, the Liverpool *Daily and Weekly Mercury*. Through the daily press he probably reached the large industrial group who most needed advice and who could not afford the expensive *Australia and New Zealand* volumes.

In passing, it might be noted that the Liverpool *Mercury*, while an important provincial newspaper, had small circulation outside England. Consequently, files of this paper are rare in the United States. There is a good run at the Harvard College Library, however, from which the present text is taken. The articles, which bear Trollope's signature, can be found on page five every Saturday from July 3, 1875, through November 13, 1875.

Trollope seems to have had two purposes in the 1875 series: first, to summarize the essential historical background material; and second, to check the colonies' development since 1871 and offer to the prospective emigrant the latest authoritative information. Thus he brings his record up to date, but adds little factual material to the earlier study. Such sketches as are found in Letters VIII and XI, however, are wholly new. But undoubtedly of greater interest to readers already acquainted with Trollope's views on Australia are Letters I–VI, written from Aden and Ceylon. Letters II and III especially are lively and charming, full of amusing observations on the oddities of foreign deportment.

The dramatic account of the savage Santa Cruz islanders' attack on Commodore Goodenough's landing party and the gallant leader's subsequent death (Letter XVIII) is in Trollope's best narrative manner and deserves a better fate than its quick journalistic oblivion. As interesting as the incident itself are the comments it evoked. Those who in thinking of England's colonial expansion conjure up a picture of the British lion growling imperialistically will be surprised at Trollope's attitude. Not only does he make clear the widespread opposition to annexation of new territories, but he shows the general reluctance to accept the white man's burden on any terms. Even the well-intentioned activities of missionaries meet with strong opposition. Exploitation often takes the shape of a new "culture," and the natives are only made restless, discontented, and embittered. It is best, one gathers, to allow primitive peoples to solve their problems in their own way. Throughout this series of articles it is abundantly evident that Trollope was vigorously anti-imperialistic, and that he observed with trepidation the inexorable circumstances that were increasing the number of peoples who looked to Britain for support and protection.

Of particular interest and amusement to historically minded Americans in general and Californians in particular are the last two letters. About Hawaii Trollope is fantastically wrong. From his estimate of 800 miles as the distance between Hawaii and California (it is 2600) to his assertion that white men could not accommodate themselves to the island's semitropical climate, there is scarcely a statement that does not need at least qualification. About California Trollope's judgments are no less surprising. He always tried to be unbiased in his criticism of American customs, but, though he had just experienced the hardships of frontier Australia, the conventional squire in him protested against inconveniences and against the American philosophy of opportunism. San Francisco is the least interesting city he had ever visited in all his travels; there is almost nothing to see worth seeing; strangers will desire to get out of the city as quickly as they can! One wonders if Trollope did not see one of the most magnificent harbors in the world. What were his thoughts as the *City of Melbourne* steamed into the

Golden Gate? According to his own account, he was digesting the news of the failure of the Bank of California. The most noteworthy sight in San Francisco, Trollope implies, is the Stock Exchange! The normal tourist, he says, "does not care to investigate the ways of trade, or to employ himself in ascertaining how the people around him earn their bread."[17] Obviously Trollope was *not* a normal tourist—in his day or ours. But the sentiment with which the squire bows himself out is the touch of nature that makes him kin to the modern transcontinental traveler, in the matter of cleanliness still hardly more fortunate than he.

Trollope's travel books are unique. They have none of the rich romanticism of Borrow, the robust geniality of Stevenson, the provincial prankishness of Mark Twain, the bitter irony of Cunninghame Graham, the saucy wit of Evelyn Waugh. They violate almost every convention of the genre. Mark Twain was pleased to observe of *A Tramp Abroad:* "I believe it will be a readable book of travels. I cannot see that it lacks anything but information."[18] It cannot justly be said of Trollope's that they lack everything *but* information, yet the patient investigator often threatens to smother the pleasant essayist. Some such thought led Hugh Walpole to describe the travel books as "frankly failures."[19] If we are convinced that the travel writer must address only a robe-and-slippers fireside audience, then the judgment is reasonable. But should not every

[17] See Letter XX, par. 2.
[18] Albert Bigelow Paine, *Mark Twain*, 3 vols., New York: Harpers, 1912, p. 650.
[19] Hugh Walpole, *Anthony Trollope*, London: Macmillan, 1928, p. 155.

author be estimated in terms of what he attempted? Trollope was a student of society and of British colonial policy. He saw the colonies chiefly as a new home for the laboring classes. One is impressed by the heartiness with which he commends the new spirit of independence which the common workingman, freed from class distinctions, enjoys. It is not too much to say that Trollope visited the various British colonies in search of a place where economic inequalities and social injustices might be alleviated, and he was not to be deterred from his purpose. In South Africa he listened quietly to proponents of various schemes, then replied, "I shall write my own book and not yours."[20] How characteristically honest and independent!

While Trollope was away on the trip which these letters describe, one of his finest novels appeared—*The Way We Live Now*. Is there not a fine appropriateness in the title as applied to his collected works? Trollope probably had wider contacts with ordinary folk than any other writer of his day. Who has described for us more accurately how they lived? The ways in which a man may earn his bread are usually commonplace, sometimes sordid. But it was never beneath the dignity of Anthony Trollope to record them. A fellow feeling for those who never had a chance led him even as an old man to suffer hardships in their behalf. In his search for a colony where industry and sobriety would give every man an opportunity to pursue happiness in his own way, the tireless traveler sought not his own pleasure, but that of others.

[20] Sarah Gertrude Millin, *The South Africans*, London: Constable, 1926, p. 3.

Letter I

THE POLITICAL condition of Italy ought at present to be more interesting to us than that of any other European state, as having so much nearer a resemblance to that of England than is to be found in any other large kingdoms, empires, and republics. And this sympathy ought to be peculiarly close because the political virtue which always ranks first with us, that of cutting one's coat according to one's cloth, is now the grand aspiration both of the Government and of the Opposition. During the session, which is still sitting while I am writing, and which will have just ceased to sit when this is published, there has been antagonism enough to stand in the way of much performance, because the ministerial majority, though numerous, has never been compact—because, indeed, it may be questioned whether the Italian deputies have succeeded in learning in a few years those parliamentary tasks with which centuries have—or perhaps have not—made us familiar. But with every party, and it may almost be said with every fraction of a party, the dominant feeling has been to get rid of the deficit, and to establish what is called the "pareggio." The pareggio in simple English is the balance of receipt and expenditure, and the passion to achieve this is so great that it has even risen to the word equilibriomania, by which scoffers imply that this passion for an equal balance is carried almost to madness. But the passion, or rather the warm determination, exists; and, this being the case, lookers-on may feel pretty confident that the object will be at last secured. When a nation, or the parliament which represents a nation, is quite in earnest on any subject such as this, ultimate success may be regarded as almost certain.

There are, no doubt, difficulties in the way. The first difficulty is a difference of opinion as to the amount of deficit. The ministers during this session have stated it at 54 millions of francs, or £2,160,000; whereas the Opposition assert that it reaches the sum of 85 millions of francs, or £3,400,000; and of course there has been hot blood as to this difference. And then when measures are proposed for producing the much desired "pareggio"—the pareggio which both sides are determined to achieve—party grounds of disagreement which we in England understand so well, will arise, and have arisen. Last session a measure was proposed for the compulsory registration of deeds, which would have gone very far to do what was wanted. A deed now is often not registered, and therefore does not pay the tax for registration, unless it is required as evidence in a court of law. When so required, then it can be registered and the tax paid; and, as a natural consequence, the tax is evaded on such deeds generally. The bill was read the first and second time, and carried successfully through all clauses. But the voting for such first and second reading and for the various clauses was open voting, and the ministerial majorities sufficed. But the Italian constitution requires that the third reading shall be carried by secret or ballot voting; and the bill on which so much depended, which had been so successfully carried through all its open stages, at last came to utter shipwreck when individual gentlemen were able to express their own wishes in secrecy! The question first asked by us would be, "Why should the constitution contain so absurd an enactment, one that has never been known to us in England?" The Italian replies that the deputy is thus enabled, once at least in the passage of a bill, to express, without fear or favour, his unbiassed opinion. No Englishman likes any strong departure from his own parliamentary usage, and it may be doubted whether this particular departure will recommend itself.

And now this session a difficulty of another kind has come—a difficulty so peculiar that no Italian statesman knows how to cope with it. Garibaldi is one of the deputies from Rome, and has descended into the arena of politics, determined to take a strong part in the prosperity of his country, as he did in its reunion and creation. But it is very hard for any minister to know what Garibaldi may regard as good for his country. They do know, however, that whatever his views may be they must be respected. The national feeling respecting him is so strong, the idolatry with which he is regarded by the populace is so perfect a worship, that it is almost impossible that they should not flatter him, and at any rate appear to agree with him. A ministry could not exist against which Garibaldi should lift his hand with a determination to

oppose it to the death. A ministry could do almost anything to which Garibaldi would give an undeviating
and determined support. Then, some may ask, why
should not Garibaldi be the minister for his country?
No man could be found less able to fill such a situa-
tion, or less willing. He is absolutely without personal
ambition, and I think I may say with almost the same
certainty, without any comprehension of ordinary political affairs. No braver man, no man more patriotic,
more chivalrously devoted to freedom, ever lived. The
attempts he made, carrying his life in his hand, leading
a small band of half-armed devoted patriots against
kingdoms with all their armies, would have been ludi-
crously quixotic had they not been altogether successful. He did more than any other man, much more even
than Cavour, to make a united Italy. But, having
done it, he has become, sooth to say, little better than
a thorn in the side of the governors of Italy. They cannot ignore him; they cannot use him; they cannot oppose him; and certainly they cannot persuade him. At
the opening of the last session he came to Rome, and
had, as all your readers probably know, a great ova-
tion. The sight of the year, the grand day in Rome, the
one thing to be remembered in 1875, was the swearing
in of Garibaldi when he took his place as deputy.
Poems were written; tears were shed; beautiful women
were moved to the strongest emotion. The people
were in ecstasies; but the ministry were at their wits'
end. What would Garibaldi do—would he oppose
them? If so, they must retire. Could he be coaxed to
give them at any rate a half-support? If so, they might

yet do their work. Might it be possible that they should carry him with them altogether? In that case they would be powerful to do all that they conceived to be good for the country. The pareggio might be attained, and great names would be won by the happy politicians who had been able to use Garibaldi as their friend.

But such happiness as this was to be looked for by no ministers. The independence of the man is complete; and his horror at all relics of the old forms of Italian government, especially at everything touched by priest-craft, so great, that a tendency towards that form of republicanism which we call "red" always prevails with him. It was not improbable that he might at once give vent to ideas subversive of all government by any ministry. He could not be bought; could not even be tempted. Flattered he might be, but never flattered into reason—never flattered away from the passion of his soul for unrestricted freedom and the annihilation of the church. What could be done with such a man? They could but treat him with a personal attention approaching to worship, and then wait and see.

Most feared, and some few hoped, that he would act the part of demagogue, and put himself forward as parliamentary tribune of the people. He has shown himself hitherto altogether indisposed to do so. But he has come forward with three schemes of his own, altogether unpolitical in their nature, intended for the material improvement of Rome and its neighbourhood—schemes of a nature which Englishmen at any rate would hardly have expected from Garibaldi, which must be altogether ruinous to the hopes of the Red party, but which are still troublesome enough to ministers here. He proposes to make a port at Fiumicino, for the use of Rome. I am told that engineers report in favour of this scheme; but then it would, of course, cost money, and at present the pareggio is the one thing necessary. Then he would irrigate a great part of the Campagna, thereby restoring a large district to fertility, and not improbably to salubrity at the same time. Money, too, would no doubt do this, and with fair financial results, after a time. But then there is the pareggio, till the accomplishment of which Italy cannot really hold up her head! But the third scheme is the one said to be dearest to his heart. By this he would so turn the course of the Tiber as to save Rome from those inundations which are at present so injurious. This scheme, however, seems to be impracticable. The channel to be cut either on the one side or the other must be from 50 to 80 metres deep, and the engineers have declared against it altogether on the score of expense. Were Garibaldi any one but Garibaldi, this verdict would suffice. But the man who took Sicily, and who took Naples, with a handful of red-shirted heroes, can hardly be made to understand that anything is impossible; and if he be offended, if he be made to think that the ministry are faineant tenants of a circumlocution office, that they are in effect little better than lay priests, then there would be woe to the ministry. A majestic elephant, if he will do your bidding and lend you his strength, how serviceable he may be! What loads cannot he carry? What rubbish cannot he remove? But if your elephant turn upon you, and trample on you, where are you? With Garibaldi, all the energy, all the majesty, and all the power are there; and that with more than elephantine power to do good. But the elephantine docility and the elephantine submission are absent.

Such are the difficulties in the way of pareggio, without which Italians feel that Italy cannot be great and equal among the great nations. For myself, I have so strong a conviction in the power of the desire itself, that I hardly doubt of its accomplishment. Given the reality of the desire, and I think there is no room for doubt. But we in England feel that, imperative as is the necessity of an equal balance between revenue and expenditure in national as well as domestic concerns, more even than this is required to make Italy all that we would have her to be. It would be invidious to insist much on minor evils where so much good has been accomplished. But there is an evil so great, that until it be abolished the country can hardly be said to be free and open for the ordinary purposes of social life. I am speaking, of course, of what must be called the system of brigandage. In Northern Italy and Tuscany it is, as far as I know, unknown. It exists in the old Roman states, to the great detriment of the country. It is rampant in Naples; and seems to be the rule of life in Sicily. The immediate consequence is that life, and commerce, and all social improvements are confined to the towns. It is not only that the natural loveliness of the country is closed against tourists. Even that would be an enormous evil, as all will feel

who know what travellers do for Italy generally. But
the brigands do not prey only or by any means chiefly
on foreigners. Were it so, the very terrors which they
have inspired would have starved them out of their
wretched trade. All travelling is subject to this curse,
and even among the inhabitants of a district safety is
to be had only by the payment of blackmail. It cannot
be necessary that any writer should enlarge on the
absolute stoppage to prosperity which must be effected
by such a practice. Then comes the question of the
remedy. That which is so clear to us is equally clear to
the rulers of Italy. What brigandage is doing for the
country—all that it will not permit to be done for the
country—is known to every Italian politician. And
there are the laws for putting it down—laws which on
the whole are very much like our own—trial by jury,
with punishment of death for murder, and imprison-
ment for life or shorter periods, with solitary confine-
ment, labour, and other inconveniences, for attempts
at murder, robbery, &c.; and efforts certainly are not
wanting to get hold of the marauders. Not only the
police but the soldiery are employed. But when the
brigand is caught, then the humanitarian feeling steps
in, and the chief consideration seems to be how he may
be dealt with most kindly. He may, naturally, be not
a bad fellow. He was born and bred to this kind of life.
He has perhaps been good to women. Something of the
romance which we still have as to Robin Hood prevails. Yorkshire juries would hardly have found Robin
Hood guilty, and Neapolitan juries are tender to their
brigands. But the witnesses are still more tender—a

tenderness which is perhaps enhanced by the memory that Robin Hood may come back to the district, and that, at any rate, he leaves the little Hoods behind him. We have known something of such tenderness in Ireland. Then there is a third seat of mercy, which, I confess, is to me less intelligible. The executors of the law, when they have got hold of their brigand—when the law, after all its perils, has vindicated itself—are again merciful. They are almost afraid to carry out sentences of death, because of the feeling of the public. This may perhaps be justified as regards the executors of the law, though lamented as regards the public feeling. For surely the first object should be to put down an evil so fatal to the prosperity of the country. But the plague, when got under lock and key, when apparently removed from further evil-doing, at any rate as far as he personally is concerned, is allowed after too short a lapse of time to reappear on the scene. The effect is that men are not afraid to become brigands. The greatest danger in their way is that of slaughter in combat; and that danger will never suffice to keep men from an employment which is dear to them.

And there is unfortunately another cause operating in favour of brigandage. I need hardly point out that there exists a passion of internecine warfare between the priesthood and the government of Italy, at any rate in Southern Italy. Italy has become Italy by setting its foot upon the neck of the church. It can hardly be expected but that the church should in all things be opposed to the government, should be inimical to the execution of all modern laws, and opposed to all modern reform. I do not know that I should be justified in saying that the priesthood is in favour of brigandage, but it is impossible but that the brigandage and the priesthood should in some degree range themselves on the same side. The brigands have faith and believe in their pastors. They do not rob their own curés. They exact no blackmail from priests. As a matter of course, the priests also believe in their brigandage. No doubt a country curé in the South of Italy will tell the men of his flock not to become brigands. No doubt he will require some penance to be done as he gives absolution. But nevertheless his sympathies on the great national question are on the same side as those of the national robber; and in individual cases he will aid the escape of the man, and by no means assist cordially in securing the evidence which is necessary for the man's conviction. The evil is so deep-seated, so inherent in the customs of the people, has been so strengthened by the political changes made in the country, as to have become perhaps the greatest difficulty in the way of a patriotic minister. But it must be stamped out before Italy can take her rank with the greater and more civilised nations of Europe.

Letter II

THE JOURNEY from the Mediterranean down through the Red Sea to Aden is not very popular among travellers. It is one of the great highways of the world, traversed with as much certainty, as great rapidity, and as quick a succession of passengers as almost any other. Those who know it well look on it as the London clerk, who goes daily from Paddington to the Bank, looks on Oxford-street and Holborn. To the Chinese merchant, the Singapore official, the Indian officer, the Ceylon coffee-grower, and the Australian squatter, it becomes, after the first journey, almost without interest. The indifference which comes from familiarity is even passed on from one to another; so that even the neophyte of the East, the lad who is going out to make his fortune, or the lass to win her husband, are taught beforehand to be indifferent to the wonders through which they will pass, and to think more of the comforts, or discomforts, of the Peninsular and Oriental ships, whether the wine be bad or the curry good, or the supply of young men for conversational purposes sufficient, than of the lately achieved miracle of Lesseps's canal, or the very ancient miracle of the tanks at Aden.

The former is not seen by those who make the first part of their journey overland across Europe to Brindisi. Such travellers still cross Egypt by railway, the passage through the canal being confined, as far as our Great Eastern Mail Ship Company is concerned, to the leviathan vessels, mostly of 3000 tons and upwards, which now leave first London and then Southampton for the East. These vessels go on through Egypt to Bombay, Calcutta, or China, as the case may be; whereas the quicker traffic which has reached the Mediterranean by Brindisi is still carried from Alexandria to Suez by railway.

As I travelled through Italy, I have not seen the canal, but, having been much interested about it during a sojourn in Egypt in its early and unfortunate days, and having then felt very doubtful whether the canal would ever be made, I was interested in learning what I could of its fortunes on the spot. With this, as with most of the great enterprises of the world, it seems to be clear that the gainers by what has been done will not be the originators, or the subsequent speculators, so much as the public at large. It has cost, I am told, £16,560,000, of which £8,000,000 were subscribed by original shareholders, and £4,000,000 by preference debentures at 5 per cent., 300 francs having been paid for 500 francs of stock. This I think means a guaranteed interest of something over 8 per cent. Then the Pasha as he was, or Khedive as he is, subscribed a sum of £3,600,000. This he seems to have done as a penalty for non-performance of his first contract to the Lesseps Company, by which he had promised the cession of a large territory—which promise the Sultan would not permit him to keep, the Sultan having been not improbably instigated in this very judicious refusal by English counsels. For this large sum of money the Viceroy is entitled to no interest. This, however, by no means includes the whole of the Viceroy's contribution to the work. Out of the eight millions originally subscribed, he holds stock to the extent of something over three and a half millions; but he has relinquished all right to interest on nearly the whole of this, in consequence of the injury supposed to have been done to the canal company in reference to their once promised territorial possessions, and as a guarantee for the payment of interest to other parties. He also waives his claim to any dividends at all, even on the small remaining amount of his stock, till everybody else has had 5 per cent. all round.

Then a further sum of £1,200,000 has been raised on delegations, as they are called, of 500 francs each, at 10 per cent., on which 270 francs were paid. These are to expire after a lapse of 25 years, unless there has been reached an amount of financial prosperity hardly to be hoped. It is in favour of the holders of these delegations that the Khedive has given up his claims on the small amount of stock which he was allowed to keep in his hands.

It will be seen, therefore, that in fact the poor Viceroy has been made to bear the brunt of the burden. In hard cash he has subscribed over £7,000,000 sterling, and for this he can never receive any money return. Nor is this by any means the whole of his loss. Previous to the opening of the canal, everything passing through Egypt, from sea to sea, was carried by the railway, and that railway was the Viceroy's property. I remember hearing, more than 15 years ago, that the Peninsular and Oriental Company alone paid the Pasha £300,000 a year for the traffic—that is, on an average to that amount. Now he has been forced by foreign interference to supply the means of carrying out an enterprise for which he will never be remunerated, and in doing so has starved an enterprise by which he was enriched. But the Viceroy of Egypt is like the rich and weak old uncle of a lavish and impoverished set of nephews and nieces. He is to pay for everything. Every man's hand—particularly the hands of every foreigner—more especially the hands of every Frenchman, are in his pocket; and it must be understood that his pocket is the Arab pocket generally. His possessions are not what he has inherited from his Viceregal predecessor, or earned by the sweat of his Viceregal brow, but all the taxes of all the country. He takes everything, and he pays for everything; and the astute foreigner of the Levant, the Frank from the West, who has found the despised Orient to be still capable of being squeezed, is not at all too proud to grow rich on the liberality of the Khedive, which of course means the taxes levied from the Arab labourer.

In this way, and by the persevering energy for which the world has now given M. Lesseps due credit, the canal which joins the waters of the West to those of the East has been made, and such ships as the Peshawur and the Pekin—of a size which was not thought of when the canal was first mooted—ride through from the Mediterranean to the Red Sea. When Mr. Stephenson expressed an opinion that the canal would never be made, he founded it, if I remember right, on a calculation that no amount of tonnage would pay for the cost; that as the capabilities for carrying were increased so also would the cost be increased. The canal has been made, and his prophecies as to the fact have been falsified. Whether the calculations on which he founded his prophecies were right or wrong we do not, I think, yet know. The grand contributor will certainly not have done well with his money, as we have seen. Whether his colleagues among the original stockholders will be ever in a good position is, I think, doubtful. The great anxiety expressed that the holders of the preference stock should get their interest is, I think, against the original stockholders.

A net revenue of a million sterling a year is required to pay the guaranteed dividends and an interest of 5 per cent. on the stock, and also to maintain the canal.

For interest . . . . £ 840,000
For the maintenance of the canal .   160,000
                                        ―――――――
                                       £1,000,000

When the tonnage was 10 francs a ton it was found that 6850 tons a day would be required to make this sum. Since that the duties have been raised to 13 francs a ton. Your readers will probably remember the efforts which were made last year by M. Lesseps and the managers to levy a still higher toll, and how a threat was made that the canal should be closed unless those who had the control in their hands would consent to such higher toll. The canal is still open, and not, I think, likely to be closed; but it may be doubted whether the required tonnage will be reached for many years. I found that a first-class Peninsular and Oriental ship paid from £1250 to £1350 for a single passage. In addition to the tonnage, a charge is made of 10 francs for each passenger carried; but the revenue from this is so small as to be hardly worth consideration. The distance is about 85 miles, and the time taken in passing, exclusive of the dark hours, is about 18 hours. During night the vessels lie still; each vessel is therefore, on an average, about 30 hours in the canal. There is room but for one vessel, but the stations at which vessels can pass are frequent, and the intercourse is arranged by telegraph wires. The work of transit is, I am assured, very well done.

At Suez I joined the ship which had come through the canal, and very soon encountered the dreaded heats of the Red Sea. It certainly is a trouble to find any thinnest amount of clothing a burden, and a sheet at night to be as heavy as a load of blankets at home. But nobody was ill, and everybody ate and drank most copiously. I cannot say that the eating is good. Meat picked up about the coasts of Italy and Egypt is apt to be tough; butter becomes disgusting; ship-tea is a bitter cross; ice is not forthcoming—why not, I cannot say, as the Americans have it in plenty on all their ships, and we also on many of ours. But still the eating and drinking is very wonderful; tobacco gives great relief; and the young ladies, freed from the conventional restraint of the drawing-room, seem to have a good time.

We entered the Red Sea at the bottom of the Gulf of Suez, and got out of it by the straits which pass into the Gulf of Aden at Perim. Perim is a little island, a miserable little island, which we are said to have got from the French, or rather to have prevented the French from getting, by a feat in jockeying. A young French naval officer, when at mess with certain English officers at Bombay, allowed a French secret to escape him. There was a little island at the foot of the Red Sea on which his captain was about to put his flag and call it France. A zealous British midshipman, not bearing the idea of such encroachment on British rights, posted off to his captain and told the story. The result was that when the Frenchmen arrived the British flag was flying. I trust, for the honour of England, the story as I have told it is not exactly true; but, if it be so, France has been amply avenged. We bear the cost of maintaining a fort on this inhospitable island. We drive one of our officers to melancholy madness by leaving him there. We supply the troops out of our poor numbers. And while Perim is in our hands any other nation will get as much advantage from it as we do. Sad stories are told about Perim. The single officer stationed there was once driven by desperation to play beggar-my-neighbour with his sergeant, and was therefore cashiered for conduct unbecoming a gentleman. The poor fellow should have confined himself to patience. Another gentleman, when his time was out, expressed his delight with the place, and asked for a second term; then for a third and a fourth. This gave rise to inquiry, and it was found that he had been all the time at his club in Piccadilly. These probably are only Red Sea tales; but the island—desolate, without a blade of grass, burnt to a cinder, with the fierce sun always raging on it, with its lighthouse and miserable garrison—is an unfortunate truth.

Perim guards the entrance to the Red Sea, and below Perim we are in the Gulf of Aden. Opposite to Perim is Bab-el-mandeb, where the French once thought to make a settlement, but failed, as was no wonder, beneath the horrors of the place. The solitary white house which they built amidst the sands is still there to be seen. But here, and indeed at points elsewhere, both above and below, the land rises close on shore in shapes which are most picturesque. The tops of the hills, or rather little mountains, are sharp and serrated, and they group themselves well amidst the blue bays of the sea. When seen by moonlight or a setting sun, they are very lovely; though even then the arid sand, the light yellow colour, the absence of all herbage, and the continuous heat, make one think of regions far from Elysium.

Then Aden is reached, which is in the same way parched, scorched, burnt, a place of cinders and fire, but still very picturesque from the combination of sharp hills, variegated outline, and little bays of clear water. The wonder of Aden is in the tanks; and on reaching [that place], I and certain friends whom I made on the voyage were taken to the tanks at once. It was moonlight, but moonlight so clear that I am prepared to say that it is thus that the tanks of Aden should be seen aright.

Aden is surely one of the most singular places in the world. There is a jutting promontory—almost an island—standing over 1700 feet out of the sea, and under this and around is congregated one of those fantastic mixtures of Oriental races which money from the West will collect whenever the West may require services to be done.[21] There are negroes from the opposite coast of Abyssinia, rowing boats and diving for sixpences. There are patient Arabs, coaling the steamers and drawing water: wood there is none to hew. There are native Jews, said to be a remnant of the lost tribe, selling ostrich feathers; and there are Parsees from Bombay—not, one would think, of the best class—keeping shops and making their fortunes. Of course with these, and over these, and as it were possessing them, are to be seen the British officers and the British soldiers for whose sake the others are all congregated. I was astonished at the size of the place and at the extent of the work that had been done. The road is not very long, but it is very good; the fortifications are not probably very strong, but they are very complete. Driving out of the town, which clusters down at the water's edge, one reaches the gate that leads into the cantonment—or, as it is called, cantoonment—in about two miles. This the unwary traveller passes without difficulty before the ill-omened hour of night, but is caught in a trap as he comes back later on in the evening without a pass. Such was our fate; but a good-natured, though perhaps treacherous, sentinel did at

---

[21] Perim and Aden have grown since Trollope's day. Census figures for 1921 show a population of 55,000.

last allow us to pass. And here he is driven through the little world of barracks in which the soldiers live. The only imposing structure seems to be the prison, which surely ought to be large enough for three Adens. On the other side of this cluster of buildings are the tanks, which, by their singular nature, their grandeur, their ancient celebrity, and their modern workmanship, as also by their apparent futility, almost defy description.

The reader must understand that no man knows or has the slightest idea when they were made. In speaking of them, men throw out suggestions as to very close descendants of Adam and Eve. The place itself is utterly waterless, and rain falls, they say, about once in three years. The earliest settlers, therefore, whenever and whencesoever they may have come, were bound to husband this rain when it did fall. Over the site of the military town there is a ravine with a rough high rocky side, with little cross ravines pierced into the mountains, and down these, no doubt, it was found that the water, when it had fallen, rushed with great violence. This was clearly the place to catch it; and that it might be caught, enormous pits were made, with openings from one into another, and so contrived that the use of the water might be economised. These pits cannot well be counted, because the stranger hardly knows where one begins and another ends; but he is told there are ten of them. They are connected by underground passages for the water, which are regulated by sluices and pumps. The sluices and pumps, I take it, are all modern; but the passages, the gangways, the flights of steps, the arches and galleries, and then the gardens, which must have cost a world of care, constitute the beauty of the place—these and the beautiful overhanging mountains. The mountains are old enough, but all [those things] which are marvellous by their workmanship both in stone and brick, reminding us of some cherished well-chiselled fortress at home, are very modern, and must have been very costly.

But I fear the tanks are almost useless. Large as they are, they contain nothing near sufficient for the supply of Aden as she is now. They are empty now—they are generally empty. The oldest inhabitant may see them filled two or three times in the course of his Aden experience; but their normal condition is one of emptiness. The real supply of water is either brought in on camels' backs in skins, or else condensed down at the edge of the sea. In all such places, condensed water now rectifies the niggardliness of nature. Nevertheless, the tanks of Aden are so wonderful, so great, so well contrived, and so picturesque, that I trust they may be long maintained by the tax-payers of Great Britain.

Letter III

ALL THE WORLD knows that the island of Ceylon is entered from Europe, and, indeed, as far as its British owners are concerned, from India and the East also, at Point de Galle, the harbour there being at the extreme south of the island, and in the direct course from Suez to Calcutta, China, and Australia. But all the world perhaps does not know that Galle is that Tarshish whence, once in three years, came the ships of Solomon, "bringing gold and silver, ivory, apes, and peacocks." Indeed, it can hardly be said that any one does know the fact; but there is much evidence to prove that it was so, and they who are learned in such matters seem now to have arrived at that conclusion. The Ophir which supplied Solomon with the gold for his temple seems to have been Malacca, which also belongs to us Britishers; and Tarshish, if Galle be Tarshish, was in the direct route from that Ophir to the Red Sea, where Solomon's ships were built.

Galle has maintained its reputation as a port with a more lasting renown than has been given to any other haven in the world; and, singularly enough, it has done so with very few claims on the score of natural advantages. It was on the direct route from Ophir to the Red Sea. It is in the direct route from Suez to Melbourne and Shanghai. But it is by no means a station worthy to be trusted by ships. It is very small, with dangerous rocks, difficult of entrance and difficult of egress, subject to currents, and a perplexing spot to the great Peninsular and Oriental Steamship Company, whose vessels have more than once suffered from these evils. But a depôt in Ceylon is essential, and none other has hitherto been practicable. The island has but one fine harbour, that of Trincomalee, which many seafaring men declare to be the finest harbour in the world. But Trincomalee lies high on the eastern coast, and is out of the way of our traffic, and hitherto we have borne to be buffeted about at Galle, as no doubt were Solomon's ships in their time. But now the beneficent authorities of the island are erecting a breakwater at Columbo, the capital, which lies on the western coast; and when that is completed, the ancient glory of Tarshish will, I think, be at an end.

In the meantime, all Eastern travellers visit Galle. It is a place in which you have all your clothes washed in six hours as you go out to China, very much to your gratification; where you buy tortoiseshell and false sapphires, and make your first personal acquaintance with rupees. It is very pretty as you enter it, the cocoanut palms coming down to the very marge of the water, and very hot—I hardly know where you shall find a hotter spot in your travels. When you land, and in truth long before you land, the traders of the place are on you with wonderful bargains. Portions of Ceylon have long had a reputation for rubies and sapphires, and you find that you have just arrived in the nick of time. A handsome commercial gentleman in a turban and petticoats unrolls for you from his bosom his pet treasure, his one really magnificent sapphire ring, and with true Oriental candour imparts to you the secret that troubles have come upon him, and that he must have money. He wants money on that very day, and will therefore let you have his one treasure—the heart out of his bosom it is, the very blood out of his veins—for any trifle of money, say £70! He tells you that you, being a man of the world, are of course aware that it is worth at least double that. You have not £70 for the gem, and then he comes down rapidly to £60, £40, £20, £10, £5; and at last he clings to you, in his despair, demanding what you will give him. You, in your despair at his persistency, offer him three half-crowns. He clutches greedily at your silver, lest you should repent, and then glides off in triumph, leaving in your hands the bit of glass set in brass. In his way he is a good industrious man, and is earning his bread to the best of his ability in the vocation to which he has been bred.

You are greeted at Galle by various Eastern races. The commercial gentleman was by descent an Arab, and is now called throughout Ceylon a Moorman. He is a Mahomedan, and on the whole a very useful industrious fellow, given to keeping shops and making money. Of course, he asks £70 when he means to take 7s. 6d. From time immemorial, such has been the nature of the trade to which his people have been accustomed. His brother in London takes off 10 per cent. from his prices if you have the effrontery to ask for it, but makes no allusion to the custom if you civilly pay your bill without reference to the disagreeable subject.

I do not know that as regards honesty there is much difference.

Then you find a lithe, well-made, tall black fellow doing all your work as you land. He carries your box, and washes your clothes, and runs alongside your horse as you drive or ride. And when you get further up the country it is he who cultivates the coffee, and is known to be the labourer on whom the success of all enterprises in the island must depend. He is a Tamil, and has come over, either in his own person or in that of his respected ancestors, from the Malabar coast in Madras. He is a Hindu, and worships Siva, and is a very important person in Ceylon, making up, with his relatives, almost a quarter of the population. His, indeed, was for many centuries the ruling race in the island, the kings of Ceylon having been of Tamil origin, though they had adopted the religion of the country they had conquered.

But the person who will strike you most is the epicene-looking person with a round comb in the head and the hair turned up behind. Although you will have heard about him before you land—for in spite of appearances it is a he—still you will take him for a woman. He is generally neat and nice to look at, though not, I believe, especially cleanly in his domestic habits. He is a Singhaleese, the real native of the island, whose written history spreads back over 2400 years, and who worships Buddha. Out of a total population in the island of 2,400,000,[22] there are in the island

[22] Ceylon now supports a population of 5,125,000, of whom only 9500 are Europeans. As Trollope predicted, Galle has lost its importance; 1927 census figures give Columbo 244,163.

1,670,000 of these Singhaleese. They are much given to agriculture, and are landowners—sometimes to the extent of a quarter of a cocoanut tree each. In the towns they condescend to wait upon their European conquerors. Very good servants they are, creeping about with noiseless tread, and understanding perfectly what you want of them, even when you do not speak their language or they yours. They are a people of many castes, and with much pride of race, having their own aristocracy, and indeed the relics of the royal blood of Kandy among them.

On landing at Galle you will also see the coloured descendants of the old European conquerors of Serendib, as Ceylon used to be called in old days, and is still described in poetry. These European conquerors were first the Portuguese, who came in 1505, and remained, sometimes with increased and sometimes with lessened dominion, till the middle of the next century. They were cruel masters, intent on money and also on masterdom, but not unfrequently failing in the pursuit of both. They never held the entire island, and were much at war with the old kings, who had established themselves among the mountains in the centre of the island at Kandy. They also had endless quarrels with the Dutch, who first came in 1602, and became masters of Ceylon in 1658. There are few material relics left of the Portuguese; but their names are still borne by Singhaleese families, among whom not a few delight to call themselves Dons. The Dutch seem only to have cared for money—that is, for trade—and became masters only because masterdom was necessary for their business. But they never owned the whole island or conquered the kings of Kandy.

Of both the Portuguese and the Dutch it may be said that they cared little or nothing for the well-being of the people among whom they had settled themselves. Nor, as we remember, did the Spaniards, who spread themselves through the western islands and continents. Nor, I fear, did the English do so in their attempts at colonisation in the reigns of Elizabeth and her immediate successors. It is probably the advance of civilisation rather than the difference of races which has produced the beneficence of the present rule in Ceylon. The Dutch remained till 1796, when the island, as far as they held it, was taken in possession by the English.

The descendants of these two races form a population somewhat exceeding 14,000, and are as easily distinguished as are the Singhaleese themselves. They are generally called burghers, though I have been informed that they do not themselves like the name. They are of European progenitors, with some admixture of native blood, either Singhaleese or Tamil. Their condition in that respect is the same as that of the mulatto in the West Indies, though probably they are nearer to their European parents than are the mulattoes. They are lawyers, civil servants in the lower grades, and clerks; but they seem seldom to rise to wealth or prominence. They are chiefly of Dutch origin, partly of Portuguese, and probably, in some degree, of English blood. Throughout the towns in Ceylon the traveller will hear and see much of the burgher, but he will not see much of him in the houses of the dominant British lord of the colony.

And at Galle the British lord will also make himself conspicuous. You, my reader, when you land, if it be your intention to remain in the island and not to pass on by the first steamer to Calcutta, China, or Australia, will, no doubt, have an introduction to some such lord. At Galle he will probably be living in Oriental luxury on a salary. He will be the master of the port, or the agent for the province, or the resident clergyman, or the officer in the receipt of customs. Perhaps the representative of the great Peninsular and Oriental Company will receive you with open arms, which means immediate brandy and soda-water and a dinner a little later on; and, till the musquitoes have found you out, you will think that no life can be more delightful than that at Galle, with white jacket and white trousers, and ever so many rupees a month.

But, as I have said before, the days of Galle as the great port of Ceylon will probably only endure till the breakwater has been made at Columbo, and then the name of Galle will become, like that of Tarshish, a word famous in history. The white trousers and the white jackets and the good dinners and the soda and brandy will all migrate, and the collector of customs will no longer complain, as he did in my case, because he is called upon to sign his name on a holiday. The town now is small, cleanly, very pretty, quaint, and still bearing in all its constructions a thoroughly Dutch air. It has now a population of 47,000 souls, and is second in importance only to Columbo itself.

Should Galle ever suffer in this fashion—and I fear that it will suffer—my sympathy will chiefly be bestowed upon the keeper of the Oriental Hotel, a hotel which I found to be exceptionally good and clean, and one in which the host or hostess—probably both—thoroughly understands the elements of a good dinner in the tropics. In these distant regions a good dinner is not supplied at a very cheap rate; but then neither are the elements cheaply procured.

When you are at Galle your first object—after having had your clothes washed—will naturally be to take yourself to Columbo, the capital. When visiting—I was going to say a foreign, but I had better say a strange country—the visitor always wishes to find himself in its very centre. There are two modes of making this journey. There is a steamer called, I think, the Serendib, which makes the tour of the island, and which is, I am told, very comfortable. But it may be tedious to wait for this. And there is a royal mail coach. In Ceylon, as in all other colonies that I have visited, the word "royal" is much beloved, and is an additional testimony to the popularity of British rule. This mail coach travels twice a day, and performs the distance, 72 miles, in eleven hours. I went by night, and I found the journey pleasant enough. It was very warm, but not unbearably warm. The coach was full, but still there was room for my legs. The pace is slow for the whole journey, but was by no means slow while we were actually going, the time being lost at the numerous stages. It seems to be impossible to imbue the minds of the normal Singhaleese with any idea of the importance of time.

Our journey was made by night, and consequently in the dark; but was, nevertheless, interesting, because it was strange. It was through palm trees the whole way, and almost through one continuous village of native cottages. We changed horses every six or seven miles, and in the middle of the night were told that supper was ready for us at the "rest-house." Rest-houses seem to be an institution peculiar to Ceylon. They are inns subsidised to a certain extent by Government at places in which it is expedient that such accommodation should be afforded, but which, without such subsidy, would not afford sufficient trade to tempt an innkeeper to establish himself. They are therefore, in a degree, Government houses, and the prices to be charged are affixed by the superior powers. A book is kept in which complaint can be made; and I presume that such book is subject to examination by regular inspectors. I was travelling with a Ceylon merchant and his family, whose acquaintance I had made on board the steamer; and this gentleman, with stern justice, reported that the accommodation afforded was not exactly what it should have been. I am bound to say that it could hardly have been worse. A hot meal with a pretentious number of dishes was set before us; but to eat of any of them was impossible. I was told afterwards that it is expedient that travellers who are particular should give notice of their coming by telegram, and that when this is done the rest-houses give ample satisfaction. As it was, we paid and grumbled, and were probably much the better for not eating a heavy supper.

All along the road, though we were travelling by night, we found natives awake and swarming in numbers. In all the cottages there were faint lights, and whenever we stopped there were slight, half-naked creatures looking at us. In the dark it was almost impossible to see whether these were men, women, or children; of the latter there were no doubt many, who with much ease had raised themselves from their couches to enjoy the excitement of the royal mail coach.

Exactly at five a.m., the prescribed time, we entered Columbo by the road across the Galle Face. I should have said that the entire road from Galle to Columbo is excellently made, and kept in excellent order. In a crown colony, such as Ceylon—which means a colony with a despotic government—roads are generally good. Columbo was all asleep as we arrived. My first question was asked as to the Galle Face, which is a broad open space—beautifully green, I was told, in pleasant weather, but now of an unlovely brown—lying down to the sea, on which ladies love to walk and gentlemen love to be with them—the fashionable esplanade of the town; but why called Galle Face I could find none to tell me.

Letter IV

AT COLUMBO I was entertained by my friend the merchant, whose house is famous for a tortoise. The tortoise was brought to that very house at the end of the
last century from some other eastern region, and was
then supposed to be the oldest inhabitant of the place
whence he came. He is now very venerable, very
lethargic, and very much respected. He moves from
the front to the back of the house according to the
monsoons, making his journeys in a very leisurely
fashion. Two or three men can stand upon him without hurting him; and altogether he is just the tortoise
to beat the hare. As he is almost the chief celebrity of
Columbo, I do not apologise for introducing him.

Independently of the tortoise, Columbo is not a
very interesting town. It has a pretty cathedral church,
a commodious governor's house, an excellent club, and
is at present very prosperous, and very hot. It is prosperous because the prices of coffee are high, and hot
because it lies low down on the seaboard. As I said before, the harbour is bad; or, rather, it has no harbour.
But this great evil is to be remedied by a breakwater.
It contains a population of 97,000, which, if the printed
return be correct, has swelled to that number from
50,000 in 1866. The former number is at any rate true.
The latter was probably guesswork.

There can be no doubt as to the general prosperity

of Ceylon at the present moment. It pays its way without difficulty. It collects a revenue of about £1,-300,000, which is ample for its purpose, and collects it without severity. There is no tendency to insubordination among the people, the chief grumblers being one section of the Europeans, who wish, as is always the case in every colony, to have things done in a manner different from that pursued by the other section. There can be no doubt of the progress yearly made by the natives both in education and wealth; and out of a population of 2,400,000, all are natives except about 24,000. It is impossible not to see that this prosperity is due to the gentleness of the present British rule, and the appreciated desire of British rulers to give the natives all the privileges of free men. Probably the most useful step hitherto taken for the good of the island at large has been the making of roads and railways.

When we Britishers first took Ceylon, the island had been reduced to a very low condition indeed by the Portuguese and Dutch, who had simply desired to aggrandise themselves and to make money. The old history of Ceylon, going back as it does to 500 years before Christ, is almost beyond our reach at present. It is to be read in Sir Emerson Tennent's account of the colony, and is written in a continuous record, which has been translated into English, and which is called the Mahawanso. Ceylon was ruled by kings at least for that entire period, and under some of those kings very noble work was done. The remains of the great cities and of the rich temples are there to this day, and in the Mahawanso is given the history of the building of these cities and temples. But the greatest work of the old kings was the making of tanks so large that they sufficed for the irrigation of enormous districts. Many of these still remaining—though remaining in ruins—are from 15 to 20 miles in circumference. "The ruins of that at Kalawesa," says Sir Emerson Tennent, "show that its original circuit could not have been less than 40 miles, its retaining band," or base for holding in the waters, "being upwards of twelve miles long." These tanks, therefore, were enormous artificial lakes, made by a prodigal use of forced labour, and were the means of providing food for millions. Ceylon is a country not rich in little streams, not rich in continual showers, but with a great fall of rain at certain periods. It became, therefore, the duty of the old kings to catch and keep the rain, and this duty they performed in magnificent proportions. As a natural consequence, the population became great. There was ample food for all. What the population was in the most palmy days of Ceylon cannot now be known, but it is presumed that rice was grown sufficient to feed three times the present number. These tanks were in the northern district of the island, and the lands which they watered are now covered with thick jungle!

This work of desolation had been commenced long before the coming of the Portuguese. From time to time, great incursions were made into the island from the coasts of India, which are but a few miles distant, and the two races, the Singhaleese and the Tamils, were continually striving for masterdom. The hands of the kings were full of war, or full of violence and intrigue, and they no longer had either time or means to maintain the tanks. The waters burst their bounds, the rice fields were destroyed, the jungle grew, and the elephants became the masters of the soil. The great cities with their temples fell into the hands of invaders—cities whose ruined monuments are equal in antiquity to those of Greece, and very much older than anything in Rome. Anurad Hapura was the royal residence of the kings 400 years before Christ, and continued to be so for more than a thousand years. And in the chronicles which tell us this there is nothing mystic. The dates of the building of every temple of which the ruins now remain are given in the Maha-wanso, that wonderful history of Ceylon of which I have before spoken. We hear of its marvels from Greek writers and Chinese travellers. It is now a dirty native village, but a village of awful ruins. Here was planted, 288 years B.C., the sacred Bo Tree of the Buddhists, and here the same Bo Tree still stands and flourishes, to the true Buddhist the most sacred spot in the world. Of the age of this tree they who have studied the subject most minutely have no doubt. Tennent says that "in all probability it is the oldest historical tree in the world." "The age of the Bo Tree," he says, "is a matter of record; its conservancy has been an object of solicitude to successive dynasties, and the story of its vicissitudes has been preserved in a series of continuous chronicles amongst the most authentic that have been handed down to mankind." The ruins of the temples here are as wonderful as the Bo Tree. They were and still are called Dagobas, and were built, of course, in honour of Buddha. I will give from Tennent the description of one as it stands at present, called the Jayta-wana-rama-dagoba:—"The solid mass of masonry in this vast mound is prodigious. Its diameter is 360 feet, and its present height 249 feet, so that the contents of the semi-circular dome of brickwork and the platform of stone, 720 feet square and 15 feet high, exceeded 20,000,000 of cubical feet." That temple was built A.D. 275, when we Britons, to whom the Singhaleese now administer with such quiet patience, had hardly as yet got out of our blue woad.

Pollanarua, which also for many centuries was the residence of the kings of Ceylon, was later than Anurad Hapura, but even more splendid. It extended 30 miles in length and four in breadth, stretching along a lake with gilded cupolas. King after king was crowned here with a magnificence which we are hardly justified in calling barbaric. It became in after years so little known, that we had been in possession of the island more than 20 years before we had found the ruins, and first heard of them by chance in 1817. These great cities, or ruins of cities, lay in the north beyond the cinnamon and the rubies and the cocoanuts, and were objects of no interest to the Portuguese and Dutch. And, long before the coming even of the Portuguese, they had been deserted by the Singhaleese and their kings, who were continually being driven south by their invaders from the Malabar coast. In the south there were mountains—the mountains of Kandy— among which was a spot almost as holy to the true Buddhist as that of the Bo Tree. It was here, on the peak which is conspicuous to every traveller in the country, that Adam set his foot when he passed over from the continent of Asia into Ceylon, and here to this day is to be seen the mark which true Buddhists believe to have been his footprint. The Singhaleese, when they were driven from their ancient capitals and rice fields, created for themselves a smaller kingdom here among the hills, and hence arose that kingdom of Kandy of which your readers have probably all heard. But, with the cities, and especially with the tanks, the population faded, and nearly half the island—and that part of the island which was most fertile—has gone back to a condition of primitive forest.

In this condition the island came into our hands; and, indeed, for some years we possessed only a portion of Ceylon, for the kings of Kandy still held their own among the mountains. In our endeavours to become lords of the entire island, some things were done by us of which we can hardly boast. We intrigued with the Minister of the Kandyan king, and got very much the worst of the intrigue; and we fought battles, in which we were not always successful. There is a sad story of one British officer who ran away, whose men were all massacred while his own life was saved, and who lived afterwards with a Kandyan wife in disgraceful seclusion. But at last, in 1820, under the governorship of Sir Edward Baines, all Ceylon, including Kandy, became ours. There was an old prophecy that Kandy could never be taken till an enemy should approach it through the earth. Sir E. Baines, who had learned enough to be aware that roads are the surest means of military as well as of commercial success, fulfilled the prophecy by making a tunnel on his road to Kandy, and in this way the enemy—or friend— that was to hold it came to Kandy through the earth.

From that day to this there has been, I think, a true endeavour on the part of the conquerors to rule the island in the interests of the natives. A Kandyan chief told the governor there the other day that the Kandyans would never rebel now, because they had all got money in their houses. The opinion was a very wise one: men who have anything to lose are generally averse to those commotions by which they may lose it.

But the mode of ruling such a people as the Singhaleese well is not always very manifest. Our British idea of ruling a people is to let them rule themselves. This clearly would not do in Ceylon. Universal suffrage, with a coloured population exceeding the white by 100 to 1, would soon lead to the desertion of the island, and the returning misery of the coloured voters. Ceylon is what we call a Crown colony, in which the governor is all but despotic, though subject, of course, to the higher despotism of the Colonial Office at home. He is assisted by an executive council, which comprises his five ministers, and a legislative council, which is made up of the five ministers, four other official servants, and six unpaid and unofficial members, who are, however, appointed by the governor; so that, even in the legislative council, he is quite sure of a working majority. Granting votes of money out of the revenue seems to be the chief work of the legislative council, and the spending of this money, for the good of the people at large, the chief work of the governor and his cabinet.

The question is how to spend the money. There seems to have been no doubt for some years that the opening up of new roads has been of all works the most desirable. There is a railway from Columbo to Kandy, with an extension up into the great coffee districts, which at present pays 8 per cent. profit, and which has undoubtedly been the source of the present mercantile prosperity of Ceylon. The distance opened is altogether 90 miles, and it may almost be doubted whether any more successful line has been made in the British dominions. The peculiarity of the traffic will be pointed out when I speak of coffee plantations, coffee produce, and coffee success generally.

But coffee is confined to a very small portion of Ceylon; and, indeed, the greater part of the island produces nothing which at present adds much to the wealth of its European masters. But as roads are forced on—and they have been forced on with great rapidity—rice fields are opened, and the people of the country are enabled to grow their own food. For some centuries past Ceylon has imported rice; but with roads and irrigation the island could grow rice for more than double its present population. The roads are being made, and now also steps are being taken to reform and again make serviceable the ancient tanks. Water is the one thing needed for Ceylon agriculture—water that shall be well under command, so that it can be husbanded in the tanks and utilized by appropriate sluices. If this can be done—and the efforts to do it have already been commenced—the jungle will give place to rice fields, as the rice fields of old gave place to jungle during the last centuries of Singhaleese and European misgovernment.

And there is another matter in which much may be done for the relief of the natives. Since lawyers came among them they have become a most litigious people. The lawyers who persecute them, and who never leave them as long as a drop of blood can be drawn from them, are of the burgher class, and are called proctors. A Singhaleese who wishes to sue his neighbour for any trifle will go to the nearest proctor and will readily promise all but the value to be obtained, for the learned man's assistance in the case; and the other litigant will not improbably make a similar bargain with the same proctor.

A native of Matara some time since had occasion to sue his younger brother in regard to a morsel of land. He first consulted the authorites as to a lucky hour, then fortified himself with arrack toddy, and went off to the neighbouring court. Here he was advised to go to a proctor. At the door of the proctor's house he stood awhile in awe, but at last was encouraged by the proctor's servant, and soon found himself in the proctor's presence. "How much will you give me?" said the proctor. As the land was worth £7, he promised the proctor £6. As this had to be paid at once, together with certain other fees, he sold his rice field for £9, and gave it to the proctor.

The case went on for three years, during which the proctor demanded and received continual presents in kind. Oranges, limes, soft jack-fruit, hard jack-fruit, rose-apples, pine-apples, yams, sweet potatoes, sugar cane, and marmalade were brought to the insatiate proctor from month to month. The poor man brought them not of his own accord, but was commanded to supply them in heavy loads if he wished to win his case. A milch cow and a she-buffalo were demanded. In his distress he had to sell his other little garden, but the proctor's requisitions were all supplied.

In due course a bull was wanted, then 100 eggs at Easter, bell-flowers to distil, chilies, plantains, and a monkey to amuse the proctor's wife. In getting the monkey, the man breaks his leg; but he does get it, and brings it. The proctor wants an additional bed, and the bed is furnished.

Then the man's wife has a child, and so has also the proctor's wife. The proctor thinks it a good arrangement that the man's wife shall come down as wet nurse. She comes down, and the proctor seduces her. In the meantime the man's own child perishes.

Five years have thus passed, during which time the proctor has been giving his services to each brother alike, at about the same rate. Our friend then loses his case, but of course is advised to appeal. He has to make up a terrible load of new presents, and the appeal is carried on. The first judgment is affirmed, and the man is then arrested and dragged away in bonds for £6, the cost of the appeal. Soon afterwards he died in gaol.

That is a story told to me as true, and believed by me to be true. It happened, indeed, some 40 years ago; but it happened under British rule; and the proctors' power of doing evil has not yet been materially curtailed. Measures, I am glad to say, are now being taken to clip the proctors' wings.

Letter V

I WENT from Columbo by the railway to Kandy. It is impossible to conceive a more picturesque line, or one that would strike the traveller with greater awe as he rises into the mountains, passing here and there round narrow points of the rocks, and crossing the ravines and mountains. As is the case in all tropical countries in which rain is plentiful, everything is full of growth, but of growth so thick as to impede instead of assisting human life. Whether this part of Ceylon was ever crowded with men, as were the northern parts of the island, I do not know. The enormous tanks by which the plains were once watered were not repeated here. And in those olden populous days, the mountains of Ceylon, which are now so much more precious than the plains, because of the coffee which grows among them, do not seem to have been much visited by the kings, till they were driven into their fastnesses by fresh invaders from India. The earliest kings of whom we know—kings who reigned as I have said, 500 years before Christ—came from India, and seem to have made Ceylon a happy country, as they certainly made her populous. But these kings dwelt, and built their temples and their tanks, in the ancient cities of the north. Then, after many centuries, came other invaders from the same coast, and the old families were driven for refuge among those hills which are now pierced by railways and cultivated almost up to their summits. At present the country between Columbo and Kandy, something over 70 miles in distance, seems, as it is traversed, to be almost all wood or jungle. One can see here and there little villages and paddy fields, and small bullocks grazing in the deep grass; but continued thick wood, which is here always called jungle, seems to be in occupation of the country. As one ascends higher, new openings for coffee, or perhaps for tea, are seen; but, if I remember rightly, there was no coffee yet in bearing between Columbo and Kandy.

At Peradynia,[23] a few miles before Kandy is reached, the railway turns off to Gampulla, called Gampola, and the coffee district. I may here remark that any amount of mis-spelling as to Ceylon names should be pardoned. Sir Emerson Tennent, who wrote the most learned book ever written on any colony, spells the same names in various ways. Whenever he had a rule, that rule has been altered now, and I found as many variations among authorities as there generally are as to time among the owners of various watches. As Peradynia—of spelling which there are many ways—was on the road to Kandy, I will take it on its road. Here are the so-called public gardens of Ceylon, which are not public gardens at all, but which form simply the most beautiful park that I ever entered. It is a land of loveliness, surrounded by the most perfect scenery which the mind can imagine. If, as some say, Eden was in Ceylon, this must have been the spot. It is a small park, something over 200 acres, surrounded in

[23] Now spelled "Peradeniya."

part by the Maha-Wella-Ganga river—the one great river of Ceylon—and filled to profusion with most lovely trees from every part of the world which can be made to grow here. The ground is broken and undulating, and on every side, through the vistas of trees, are to be seen glimpses of mountains and the sides of hills running steep up from the river. In the centre of the park lives, in a pretty cottage, Mr. Thwaites, the curator of the so-called gardens—surely a happy man, if there be one to be found anywhere, and not as yet driven out of Paradise. I am told that Mr. Thwaites does not care for flowers, and flowers could not improve his place. In rich growth of unequalled shrubbery and beauty of close views it cannot be beaten, and those are the matters which are dear to the mind of the curator. I told him my opinion as to the effect, and he pardoned my ignorance in regard to the things which had caused it.

Kandy, from whence I was driven to Peradynia, is in importance, though by no means in population, the second town in the island. Galle, at the south, has 47,000 inhabitants, and is visited by almost every European coming to and going from the island. Jaffna, in the extreme north, has 34,000 inhabitants, and is never visited by Europeans, unless by those who are taken thither by official business. Kandy has less than 17,000 inhabitants, and lives and is known by its own reputation. It is among the mountains, and therefore popular. It is clean and pretty, and is honoured by one of the governor's residences, of which he has three on the island. This is called the Pavilion; that at Columbo, the Queen's House; and that higher up in the mountains, at Nuwara Elliya, the Cottage. Of these the Pavilion is the most popular, and certainly the prettiest. It is hard to conceive a prettier gentleman's residence. And then, it is not the state residence, and permits of certain semi-privacies which must be dear to a governor's heart.

At Kandy is now the great Buddhist temple, containing the great tooth of Buddha. The temple is a comparatively modern affair, as is everything at Kandy, when compared with the real antiquities of this island, for Buddha and the rest only went to Kandy when they were driven from the regions below. It is a low, shabby place, with an outside building, and an interior sanctum, or centre building, in which the tooth is kept. It is opened twice or thrice a-day for religious services, which consist of meditation and the offering of many flowers. I saw the flowers, but not much of the meditation. There was a crowd of men, with some few women, gathered about the place, but one could not guess from their manner that they had come there with any purpose of religion. The head of the temple—not a priest, but a civil guardian, a man of high family, selected for the office, with a salary, and rank and privileges—met us by appointment, and was very civil to us. He could not go the length of exposing the tooth itself to our eyes, for that, I was told, was only done for royalty. This I did not quite believe, as I heard of people who had seen the tooth who were less than royal. But, for myself, I was very glad to be saved the trouble of having the long operation of unpacking done before my eyes in a place as hot as an ordinary oven. The jewels, which are real, are kept outside, and those I was allowed to see. The tooth, which is very far within, is not real—and if real, if the undoubted tooth of Buddha, would not have given out its essence of reverence to eyes so irreverential as mine. Such tooth of Buddha as the old Singhaleese possessed was certainly carried away captive to India, and was there pounded to dust in a mortar by certain Portuguese priests, who thought it incumbent on them as Christians to refuse even the enormous money bribe which was offered to them for the restitution of the opposition idol.

The tooth is suspended, under various coverings, of which the visible outside covering is a silver gilt bell—or frame, such as that of a bell—about three feet high. It is just like a church bell of small dimensions. But this is decorated profusely with ropes of jewels, which put one in mind of Lothair.[24] It is too barbaric to be beautiful, but it is enormously rich. I have said that though the tooth is false the jewels are real—I presume them to be real. I think they were most of them real till quite the other day; they were probably all real till not very long ago. Then the opportunity for selling jewels was less than now. The general desire of the world at large for such jewels was hardly known; nor the way of communicating with the world at large. Perhaps there was a higher spirit of reverence among Buddhists as well as Christians. That gentleman who showed me the gems cannot sit there always and watch

[24] See Disraeli's novel, *Lothair* (1870).

himself. Though sure no doubt of himself, he cannot be quite sure of all those about him. The thing seemed to be so easy! and then there are rumours that every jewel there is not quite what it ought to be.

We are told that even the guardian of the temple cannot open the shrine except in company with certain other minor servitors in the temple. It seemed that those around him were simply his servants, obeying his orders. There was one Buddhist priest looking on, a man draped from head to foot in yellow, and whose physiognomy was more against him than that of any other Singhaleese that I saw—a horrid cutthroat-looking fellow. But the character of the Buddhist priests generally is very low. There is one now waiting execution as a murderer—having murdered his Pandarus for undue interference with his Cressida.

The other great lion at Kandy is Lady Horton's walk—that, and an artificial lake which ornaments the town. Lady Horton was the wife of a late governor; and is very worthy of praise if she made—or caused to be made—the walk which bears her name. It is over the line and winds about among the trees and round the mountain-top, and gives a magnificent view—at one side upon the river, and at the other towards the distant coffee grounds.

I found that people at Galle and Columbo accused Kandy of being hot. It is hot. Ceylon is all hot. And Kandy, though high among the mountains, is not very high, and lies in a dip among the mountains. In all tropical regions an accusation of heat between places betrays jealousy, as among ladies does an accusation of age. No doubt it can be hot at Kandy; but, taking it throughout the year, I should think it to be the pleasantest place of residence in the island.

From Kandy I went up to Nuwara Elliya,[25] which is pronounced Nuralia, and had better be accepted by my readers in that form. This is the spot best beloved in Ceylon by the European inhabitants, and it is here that they make their holidays and run for that period of fresh air which everybody now expects to get in the holiday season of the year. It is 6420 feet above the sea, and is only 2000 below the summit of Pedro Talla Galla, the mountain with the highest summit in Ceylon. Nuwara Elliya is of course cool in the hot season; but it can also be very rainy, and is much given to storms. No one, I fancy, would like to live here all the year through.

I found considerable difficulty in getting to the place at all, as traffic by horse carriage or by horses had not yet reached a stage of much excellence in Ceylon. I went by rail back to Peradynia, and thence to Gampola, the commencement of the coffee district. On the subject of coffee I will say a few words in my next letter, but at present we will go on to Nuwara Elliya—were I actually to spell the word in any other way, no Singhaleese of any race, from the governor down, would ever forgive me. There was a coach which was to carry me 24 miles on my journey, having five hours allowed for the purpose, but which was in a chronic state of breakdown for the first half of the journey. We had three drivers; the first a Singhaleese,

---

[25] Now a famous health resort. The name is spelled "Nuwara Eliya."

the second a European, and the last, who really knew what he was about, a Tamil. By far the worst was the European, who continually told me that the whole concern was destroyed by those —— natives, and who in every difficulty threatened to knock them down, of which threat I am bound to say they took no notice whatever. To have one black fellow running along the road giving outside assistance, whether by thrashing the horses or otherwise, is usual; and when things go smoothly, and each horse's groom trots awhile by him in his own peculiar costume, the effect is rather good; but here there were generally three, and things did not go smoothly, and the poor horses were punished dreadfully, and the thing was very bad. But an end also came of that, and the coach terminus was reached at last. The evil of this, however, was that I had to travel the last dozen miles in the dark, that I lost my guide, that it rained hard, and that on an unknown and unseen road amidst the mountains, on a road winding round a precipice half the way, I almost gave myself up for lost, and thought that my bones would be pecked by unclean insects in a Ceylon jungle. But I weathered also that danger, and did reach Nuwara Elliya at last.

Here I found a regular little England, enjoying itself in its holiday. Cricket-matches were going on, and there were kinds of football. It was a race-meeting week, and the place was full of races. I soon came to know the names of the owners, the colours of the riders, and the weights. I am bound to say that the colours selected were rarely those named, and that the circumstances of the occasion generally induced the riders to put up about a stone more than the handicapping required. I don't know that the races were the worse, except that one old gentleman, who had his eyes about him, seemed to win everything. The racing was generally at eleven or twelve, after breakfast; but early in the morning we turned out and hunted the elk. I say we, because one morning I attended on a pony. There was a joint pack of beagles and Scotch greyhounds—seekers and seizers, they are called in appropriate Singhaleese sporting language—and they certainly did find a deer, and the music of the beagles through the wood was very pretty. On that occasion they did not kill their game, but I believe that they generally do so. After the races there was cricket, if it did not rain, which it always did. Then came a morning dance in the public room till dinner, and in the evening a ball, which brought the votaries of pleasure well round to the next morning's hunt. There seemed to be no rest, except on Sunday, when a good deal of sleep was done, both in and out of church. Such was the Tymkhana week at Nuwara Elliya. Of the spelling of this word I am not certain, but it signifies the great holiday festival of the year.

The place itself is certainly a very lovely spot, and a great deal is being done to increase its loveliness. An artificial lake has been made by damming a river, and beautiful walks—perhaps as delicious walks as I ever saw in my life—have been opened up through the neighbouring jungle. The spot consists of a valley, of which the surrounding summits are not high enough above it to keep the winds from it. I mounted Pedro—to mount which from Nuwara Elliya is an affair of no difficulty—and could look abroad through all the mountains of Ceylon. Adam's Peak—which, as I have said before, is the holy mountain—is nearly a thousand feet below it, but is really difficult to ascend. Any old lady on a donkey—if there were a donkey in Ceylon—might go up Pedro Talla Galla. From year to year new residences are added to this place—bungalows, as they are always called—and it is becoming a mark of recognised Singhaleese-European propriety to spend at any rate a fortnight in every year at Nuwara Elliya. The merits of the place have done much for it, and viceregal favour has completed the matter. I went there to spend a week with my very old friend the present viceroy, and a pleasant week I had.

From Nuwara Elliya I traversed the mountains to the coffee districts of Dimbula; but of Dimbula, and the coffee districts of Ceylon generally, I will speak in my next letter.

Letter VI

WHAT TEA IS to China or wool to Australia; what cotton is to the Gulf States and cotton goods to Manchester; what matrimony is to the mother of a family, and the endowed church to a country clergyman—that to Ceylon is coffee.[26] It is the salt of its life. It is not that Ceylon produces nothing else, or that it produces nothing else in excellence and abundance; but coffee is its mainstay, and, to the coffee-planter, the apparent reason of its existence. It is suited excellently for the growth of rice; it teems with the cocoanut tree; it was celebrated of old for its cinnamon, which to the Dutch was its great attraction; it will probably some day be as famous as Peru for its quinine, no plant thriving better in the island than the cinchona; it has its ruby fields and its sapphire fields, and its pearl banks. But the prosperous Ceylon merchant of the present day and the prosperous Ceylon planter believe in coffee. Coffee is up, and from day to day the sides of new hills are denuded of their old forests to make way for the coffee plant. Happy is the man who can get 300 acres of coffee ground on any terms. Blessed is the man who got his 300 acres before the late rises in the price. Contented should be the lad who can ever get his foot on a coffee plantation.

---

[26] In 1880 the leaf disease completely destroyed the coffee industry. Ceylon then turned to the cultivation of tea. Now, however, rubber, coconuts, and rice are the chief exports.

I do not know that I should gratify your readers were I to supply them with the coffee statistics of the island. A man should be tolerably well acquainted with a subject before detailed statistics will interest him, and they who are so acquainted will probably know more than I can teach them. It will be better, perhaps, that I should tell them, having so lately seen the thing with my own eyes, that the coffee-planters of Ceylon at this moment are enjoying that exuberance of triumph which a full tide of commercial success always brings with it. The coffee-planters, and the curers and manufacturers of the coffee, and the coffee-shippers, are all agog. Prices which three or four years ago would have been magnificent are now insignificant. Ninety shillings per cwt. was then a heaven of glory, whereas now the minds of coffee heroes soar to a hundred and twenty. "If you have a few thousands, you can't do better," one young man said to me, kindly endeavouring to assist a stranger in the world. I think he could not have observed my grey hairs as he was suggesting that I should commence this late making of my fortune by the purchase of a forest-clad mountain, so that I might strip it, plant my coffee, and begin altogether from the beginning. Such beginnings are being made on all sides. The lovely sloping forests are going, the forests through which elephants have trampled for we do not know how many more than 2000 years; and the very regular but ugly coffee plant is taking their place.

It must be acknowledged that the coffee interest of Ceylon, if under that name I may combine all the classes employed, deserves its present success. The energy displayed has been great, and it must be borne in mind that money expended on fresh coffee ground does not give a return at once. The land must first be bought and paid for. The mountains are generally crown land, having belonged to the old kings of Kandy, and having become ours by right of conquest. It may be as well to observe here, that all other lands in Ceylon than those thus acquired have been, as far as Great Britain is concerned, allowed to remain in the hands of the old owners, whether those owners were individuals or public bodies. A great deal of land was, at the time of our conquest, in the hands of the Buddhist priests—or rather in the possession of the Buddhist temples; and this holding still remains.

But to go back to the embryo coffee-planter. He must buy and then cut down his forest, and must, after that, burn it on the ground; then he measures out his ground in holes, and plants his shoots. He has no return till two years after that, and no remunerative return till the third year. He must, therefore, be out of his time and out of his money for four years; and who ever knows what may happen within such a space of time as that? Brazil and Java may have overstocked the market, and coffee have gone back to some contemptible ninety shillings, odious to the mind of the aspirant planter.

I passed from Nuwara Elliya into Dimbula. Now, Dimbula is a great coffee valley, and I was assured that I should see coffee there in all its glory. I received an invitation from a young planter of a noble name and race—for it is not the Johnsons and Thomsons, nor the Smiths and the Browns, who now monopolise the rich things of so gracious a land as this—and to his bungalow I went, accompanied by a future young general, who in these peaceful days is contented to serve his country semi-civilly in Ceylon. It had been one of my grand desires to see an elephant—a real wild elephant—and perhaps to shoot one. The shooting I found rather out of the question, unless I could come across the animal in somebody's cabbage garden, an edict having gone forth that elephants shall not be shot unless trespassing; and I was told that I could hardly hope to see one unless I extended my travels further than was my purpose; but on this occasion, if fortune had favoured me in the least, I might have seen an elephant afoot in his native pastures. We heard the rush of the brute close to us—within thirty yards, I should say—crushing his way through the jungle, and flying from us down the steep mountain side. The growth was so thick that we could not catch a glimpse even of his tail. I, having heard that lone elephants are rogue elephants, and that they will turn upon a man and trample him, looked about for a tree to climb. My friend, who was sportsman as well as soldier, rushed after the brute, but only for two yards; the impenetrable jungle made pursuit impossible, and, could he have caught the flying animal, he could hardly have captured him with his riding-stick. The circumstance, however, added some hilarity to our journey, and made me feel sure that there still are elephants in Ceylon.

On our route, after passing through the jungle, we

first came to a new plantation that had been planted with tea. There are those who think that Ceylon has before it a future glory in tea quite as great as that already achieved in coffee. I know no reason why it should not. That it grows very good tea I can bear witness, but hitherto it has not been grown much; the industry is as yet in its infancy, but the infant is making itself heard with a strong and virile voice. At present Ceylon-grown tea is dearer in Ceylon than tea grown in China.

Then, from the tea, we came down upon unintermittent coffee for mile after mile. The extent of acreage under coffee in the country gives to the mind uneducated in coffee generally but a faint idea of the magnitude of the crop. An Australian wool-grower, when he hears that in all Ceylon there are about 250,000 acres of coffee, and when he remembers that he pastures his own sheep over as large a surface, will not think much of Ceylon coffee. But it should be borne in mind that the whole process is horticulture rather than agriculture, and that a coffee plantation consists of a collection of shrubs each one of which is annually manured and handled and pruned, for the irrigation of which special arrangement has to be made, and which is treated as delicately and with as much care as a peach tree in an orchard house at home. If this be remembered, then 250,000 acres of coffee bushes will look large to the imagination.

I found that an extent of ground varying from 200 to 400 acres formed the model plantation which could be well managed by one superintendent. The labour question is of course the question. The Singhaleese as a rule do not work on the coffee plantations, nor I think elsewhere in similar operations for European hire. They are great as agriculturists; but then they are great also as land-holders. They love to till their own paddy fields, to own their own cocoanuts, and to live as their fathers lived before them. They are to be found in all the towns acting as servants in families; but then they generally have other servants under them. You order a Singhaleese boy—everybody who does anything for you is a boy—to get your bath ready. But the Singhaleese orders a Tamil Coolie to pump the water. A Singhaleese valet takes away your boots, but a Tamil Coolie cleans them. The work on the coffee plantations is almost altogether done by labour from the Malabar coast. These labourers are either newly imported, or are the descendants of those who came to the country long ago. But as the coffee acreage increases, new gangs of labourers are continually imported. The planter makes his bargain with some Tamil gangsman, some leader well known and well trusted in his own country; and the man, receiving from the planter a considerable sum of money in advance, goes back to India for new hands, leaving probably some formerly collected band, as it were, in hand for the advance. He invariably returns with his men. He is paid for his operation by receiving one half-penny a day for every hand under him, which is paid by the planter. The work of this man seems to be confined to keeping his men together, and seeing that they come into the field in the proper numbers. Under him there are other gangsmen, who look to the individual working of small numbers, perhaps from 20 to 30 each—and these men are paid by the planters a penny a day for each hand supervised. The male labourers receive on an average 9d. a day, and the female 7d. In this way the labour is supplied, and generally suffices. But there are times, especially when the picking comes on quick, in which the planter has to look about him; and at this time there may perhaps be a little jealousy as to the possession of gangs. A gang will sometimes wish to leave a plantation; but it is not considered to be "good form" to take a body of men from another plantation without fitting cause assigned.

The coffee up at the plantation is subject to many operations. Of course it is propagated, grown, and picked there. It then has the form and colour, and apparently the substance, of a small ripe cherry. It is pulped and skinned and dried at the plantation. But it is manufactured after it has been sent down to the town and committed to the hands of the merchant. It is again skinned and again dried; it is divided into sizes, and every bean is picked. The wonder is that it should be bought for 1s. 6d. in London after all the trouble that has been taken with it.

The planter lives a free and jolly life, as planters do almost always. Perhaps it may be a little monotonous, as his territory is small and the thing grown is only one. It is all coffee—coffee up to the verandah, coffee down to the barbecues, coffee in every twist of the hills, coffee in every bared valley. Coffee, as I have said before, is not in itself beautiful. The planter seizes probably on one of the most lovely spots on the earth for his operations; but he does not improve the aspect of it. The shrub itself is pretty enough at all times, but it is not allowed to bear luxuriantly, and the dry red earth is always visible through it. The land must not bear a weed, not a blade of grass, that is thought worthy of producing coffee. Looking down from a height the stranger will at first think a plantation fair enough to the eyes; but when he is among the sunny paths with the soil itself close to his eyes, the red-hot soil, he will hardly long be fascinated by the look of the place. The bungalow stands probably in the middle of the plantation, and here the master is informed, a few minutes after six in the morning, how many hands have been mustered to the work for that day. At four the labours of the day are over; but it is to be remarked that the Tamil labourer works throughout the day without rest or food. What he wants in the morning he takes before six, and then wants nothing, or at any rate asks for nothing, till he goes home at four to cook his rice and curry. These men live in little villages on the plantations, which are called the Coolie lines; and at no great distance, on the nearest high-road, there is always a Coolie bazaar, in which the Tamil labourers make their purchases.

A coffee-planter, I think, should be married; I do not understand how otherwise he is to get through his evenings. That theory of working all day and reading the History of England or other improving book, with a teapot before one, till bedtime, has never held water yet. At home it leads to billiard rooms and clubhouse luxuries, or relieves itself with theatres and music halls. It does so unless other special provisions be made for the amusement of youthful workers. But there are no theatres and no clubs among the bungalows, and I do not see what provision is possible between brandy-and-water and the History of England—unless a man be married.

From Dimbula I had a wretched journey back to Columbo; wretched chiefly because I was ill, and then because the carriage that was to take us did not come in time, and when it did come could not be got up the hills. I am bound to say that a truly paternal governor in Ceylon should look to the conveyances. Where everything else is so luxurious, a man feels it hard not to be able to move. I was so unwell that I telegraphed down to Columbo for a doctor to meet me there; but when I reached the place and found the doctor, I was well.

Though I have spoken so much of coffee, it is not to be supposed that the island thinks of nothing else. There are many Singhaleese to whom coffee is nothing, who perhaps have hardly heard of it; for the growth is confined to a small district lying round Kandy. A height of about 4000 feet from the sea is necessary, which altitude may perhaps be taken with a difference of 500 feet on either side; and as the country round Kandy is the only mountainous district, so also is it the only coffee district in the island. The cocoanut is the plant of which the Singhaleese is most proud, and upon which he is enabled to live almost exclusively. What can be done with the cocoanut for the purposes of general trade may be seen at the steam mills of Messrs. Leechman, in Columbo, where the fruit of the nut is turned into oil and the husks into cords and matting. Perhaps nature has produced on the earth no more famous plant than the cocoanut; and if Ceylon were to take one tree as its emblem—the Ceylon which is the island of its native proprietors more exclusively than of its British conquerors—it should be the cocoanut tree, and not the coffee plant.

Letter VII

POOR WESTERN AUSTRALIA—Swan River, as it used to be called—is a colony that has received, and I fear is likely to receive, very little attention from the British public at home. It has not sent home gold nor wool in large quantities; nor has it produced wheat sufficient even to feed itself. It has no irresponsible autocratic Parliament of its own, the leaders of which can be made knights, with ever so many letters after their names, by a flattering Secretary of State at home. It has but 25,000 inhabitants, whereas the other Australian colonies all count their people in six figures, and Victoria lives in the hope of adding a seventh in the course of a few years. And then Western Australia is still contaminated—widely contaminated—by a convict element. As a consequence, the poor little colony is not only looked down upon and despised, but it is denied the probability of rising into comfortable eminence. And yet, with the exception of the Canadian Dominion, which is now one of the biggest kingdoms in the world, Western Australia is the largest of our colonies. It is about eight times as large as Great Britain and Ireland. You may travel 1200 miles through it from north to south, and 800 miles from east to west—if you can find the means of locomotion. Had the soil and climate been together capable of producing wheat, it might have been a second United States by this time, have counted its people by millions, and have annexed all the interior of the continent, which is now claimed by South Australia. But it can produce wheat only in small patches; and as it has not yet shown itself to be possessed of other sources of wealth, it is still a poor place, in which men struggle, and perhaps only half struggle, because the wished-for prosperity seems to be so far distant.

The paucity of its products, and the apparent difficulty of drawing sustenance from the land were, no doubt, the primary causes of failure at the Swan River. But to these was added, after a while, an institution certainly evil in itself, which is now felt to be a very curse, but which at the time was regarded as a possible salvation, and which I do believe did at the time save the young colony from perishing from actual inanition. The colony was founded in 1829, when neither Victoria, South Australia, nor Queensland had an existence. News was brought home in 1827, by Captain Sterling, of a good climate and of fitting land at the mouth and along the shores of the Swan River, on the western shore of the then but little known Australasian continent, and ships were sent out by enthusiastic hopeful colonists, with men and means for beginning a new agricultural life in that distant region. In what had been hitherto done in this new world, Government had taken the lead. Government had, indeed, as yet done everything, actuated simply by its desire to get rid of its criminal population. Hanging had become unpopular. Cheap gaols, almost as fatal as the gibbet, had been condemned. As the population increased, so did the criminals; and it was thought that if they could be sent away to this world that had been found at the other side of the world, there these strong but mutinous citizens might be so handled that more good than harm should come of them—or, at any rate, whatever harm they did would not be done to us at home. In this way, and for this purpose, New South Wales and Van Diemen's Land were founded, and there—especially in the latter colony, which is now called Tasmania—convict labour was found to be very useful. Convict labour is free labour, and with the labour came also the blessing of a large Government expenditure. A convict establishment requires many officers—controllers, superintendents, doctors, chaplains, warders, &c. And these officers live and spend their salaries in the colony which is blessed by their presence. Seeing all this, and feeling that under any other probable circumstances the fate of inanition must be at hand—but still hating the idea of convicts—poor Western Australia yielded itself to its destinies in 1849, and applied to the Government at home to send it convicts. In order that he may understand the humiliation of this, the reader must bear in mind that at this time the other colonies had repudiated or were repudiating convicts. They, who had grown and become strong by convicts, had refused to receive more, and their refusal had been respected—or was in the way to be respected. In 1853 even Van Diemen's Land had received her last convict. It was therefore a very bitter pill. The suggestion had been twice rejected by the colonists before it was finally adopted. It was rejected at first with scorn, then with courage, and at last adopted in despair.

The convicts came, and with them all their salaried officers. No doubt they were of service—of such service that the colony lived, which without them would probably have perished. Roads were made; buildings were erected; money was spent. In all, 10,000 convicts were sent to the Swan River between 1849 and 1868, the total present population being only 25,000; and these were all men—as many men as would in an English town be required to make up such a population. Of course the convict element prevailed and does prevail. After a while, women were sent out at the expense of the home Government to become the wives of such of these men as were in a condition to take wives. Complaint was made that the women were not of the best class; but it may be a question whether women of the best class would have suited the purpose. But it could not be that with such immigrants the colony should bear a high moral character. But still there were the sinews, and the sinews were compelled to work; and by these means Swan River was enabled to hold its head just above the water.

The system was brought to an end in 1868, not because Western Australia, as it was then called, had become tired of convicts, but because the other Australian colonies complained of the vicinity of neighbours so disagreeable. Victoria and South Australia alleged that the ticket-of-leave men from Perth and Freemantle, towns on the Swan River, escaped into the borders, and there made themselves disagreeable. It may be that there was some touch of prudent virtue in this. South Australia had never been disgraced by British convicts, and Victoria had been equally clean since she had been Victoria. They looked down from a great moral altitude on their poor soiled sister, and expressed their indignation so loudly that the mother country was obliged to desist. As your readers are probably aware, England has now to keep her convicts at home as best she may—and Western Australia has to expiate her degradation as best she may.

There are still convicts in the colony—at this time, I believe, about 1500—the remnant of the 10,000; and there are ticket-of-leave men to a much greater number, working for their bread in different districts. The headquarters of the establishment is at Freemantle, capable of holding 850 men, and when I was there three years ago it had 360 inmates. Freemantle is at the mouth of the Swan River, eight miles from Perth, the capital. Of course the result of all this is that the great body of labourers in the colony either are convicts or have been convicts, or that they are in some way connected with convicts—and, as a further necessary result, working men are shy of the place, because, when there, they are liable to the suspicion of having been sent there under discreditable circumstances. It will be easily understood that this should tell very strongly against the progress of the place.

But, in spite of this evil, I do not know that any colony offers better terms to a working Englishman with his family than does Western Australia, or that there is any land in which such a man can expect to do better, provided he will work hard, that he is sober, and that he can place himself in the colony. Land has been offered on cheap if not profitable terms to immigrants in all these colonies, but the small agriculturist has generally met with great difficulty in selecting his land. This selection has too generally been made in a fashion which has created internecine enmity between the small owner of land, whose business it should be to grow corn, and the large holder of crown lands, whose business it is to grow wool or rear cattle. Of these feuds I may probably say something when writing of the other colonies; but there has also been this evil result from the chance and arbitrary selection made in the other colonies—that the men selecting land have not been brought sufficiently together to form helpful communities. The farmer who is twenty miles from his next neighbour, and without a road to reach even him, can hardly sell his produce. He must eat what he grows, and will have no money to buy anything else. By the last land law passed in Western Australia, which is now three years old, the free selector may take up land chosen for special occupation, on very favourable terms. This land will have been so chosen because it is supposed to be fit for agricultural purposes. The intending immigrant must not suppose by this that he will be able to enter upon land through which he can at once run his plough or work with his spade. The land will be timbered, and he must clear it. There is very much such land in Western Australia which when so cleared will not bear corn; but there is some that will. It is presumed that the land selected for special occupation will be of this quality. In some districts the land is very good, and farmers have thrived well, although the system of farming is as bad as can be. Manure has been unknown, and the same crops have been taken off the same land year after year; and yet the farmers have thrived. The terms now offered are these: The selector shall pay only 10s. an acre for the freehold possession of his land—the ordinary price throughout Australia is 20s.—and of this price he will be required to pay only 1s. an acre, each year, for ten years. If during those ten years he shall have fenced in the whole of his land, and tilled a quarter of it, then the land will be his own. In this way he may purchase any number of acres between 100 and 500, but he cannot on these terms purchase less or more. He has, however, another great advantage offered to him; for every adult person he brings with him—including, of course, himself—he has given to him 30 acres free. A man with his wife and two adult children would thus receive 120 acres. It is computed that this is tantamount to giving the immigrant a free passage, as £15 is about the cost at which he would carry himself to Western Australia.

When in the colony the other day, I heard that 400 immigrants had just arrived, or were just arriving, with the purpose of taking up land on these terms. For their passage the Government had paid, thereby conferring on them beforehand the value of the land which would have been due to them had they exported themselves. As to the labouring man, the cost of a passage out is of course the first grand difficulty of emigration. It is to be hoped that this system may be found to answer. It is open to one great objection. The immigrant who has been landed free of cost in the colony may at once take himself off to some other colony (in quest of gold, for instance, in Victoria), and have thus made poor Western Australia a dishonest stepping stone to the fruition of other desires. If, however, a strong man with a healthy family can find his way to Western Australia, and will take up land on the terms described, I think he will do as well as may be possible to him in any colony. But he must not be a man intending to have his work done for him by the payment of wages. Such a one had better not try Western Australia.

Here, as in all three colonies, wool has been hitherto the staple produce. But wool-growing in this colony has been but a poor business. It boasts altogether something less than 700,000 sheep, individual squatters owning perhaps 4000 or 5000 each. On the other wool-growing colonies 20,000 is but a small number on a single sheep run, whereas the large squatters will own from 150,000 to 300,000 sheep. In fact, the West Australian wool-grower is not a man of much account among Australian squatters generally. One reason for this failure is to be found in the poisoned bush of the country—a bush which is injurious to cattle, and absolutely fatal to sheep. This grows here and there, in patches, but in patches frequent enough to interfere materially with the growth of wool. Here, as elsewhere in this part of the world, the great panacea for all evils, the grand hope of all aspirants, has been gold. If only gold would turn up, then Western Australia would hold its own with her sister colonies, and get the better of her disgrace, and overcome her poverty, and govern herself with that independence, bordering on arrogance, which the Australian statesmen generally have been able to display. And why should not Western Australia have gold among her rocks and gullies as well as Victoria or New South Wales? Some years ago a great gold-conjuror was sent for, and, having been duly paid for his wisdom, told them that gold would certainly be found in a part of the colony north of Perth. No one who has not seen it can understand how continual and how detrimental is the hankering after gold in an auriferous country. It upsets the minds of men with a propensity for gambling, and induces them to waste their honest earnings in the pursuit, with a lavish extravagance which soon reproduces poverty and distress. In Western Australia, hitherto, there has been only the hankering, and none of the fruition. Men have never abandoned the hope. What are called signs of gold—what might, perhaps, justly be named the mark of the beast—have from time to time been found. There has never been a settled understanding, as there is with us in England, that, in whatever way a man may make his fortune, he cannot do so by picking gold out of the ground. Now, at this moment, new golden hopes have arisen. It is said that auriferous quartz has been discovered, and crushing-mills have been put up in the southern district of the colony, about thirty miles from Albany, the southern port. Gold has, no doubt, made many countries, notably California and Victoria in our day; and, as gold may still be the making of Western Australia, one ought to hope for success to the enterprise. Had I heard of new immigrants producing heavy crops of wheat, I should have been more hopeful.

I ought not to conclude these few words about this little-known colony without saying that the tribes of aboriginals are more numerous here, and stronger, than in other parts of Australia. The men and women are, I think, physically superior to their brethren in the east, and certainly seem less inclined to get rid of themselves and to die out of the land. They are a wretched hideous race, but apparently good-humoured, and on certain occasions ready to work for immediate good results. It may be that their permanence in the land is due rather to the small number of their invaders than to any strength of their own. When the country was first settled they were very troublesome, as we in our power used to consider them, by which we implied that for a time they fought resolutely for what they knew to be their own, and of which we were as resolute to deprive them. Now they are not often pugnacious, at any rate in the immediate neighbourhood of our settlements. As to civilising them, that, I think, all who have watched them know to be hopeless.

Letter VIII

THREE YEARS AGO I wrote a book about the Australian colonies, in which I thought that I praised them very much. I admired so much of what I had seen, and had disapproved of so little; I had become so thoroughly convinced of their general well-being, and entertained so few fears as to their future; I regarded the whole enterprise as being so healthy in its tendency, that it was, I thought, impossible for me to write otherwise. And I am sure that I did speak well of the colonies, and especially of Victoria. Looking back at the beginning of one of the chapters there written, I find these words—"I dislike the use of superlatives, especially when they are applied in eulogy; nevertheless, I feel myself bound to say that I doubt whether any country in the world has made quicker strides towards material comfort and well-being than have been effected in Victoria." I was almost ashamed of the general patting on the back which I had given to my friends out here, fearing that it would be taken for flattery, but consoling myself with the assurance that I had said no more than I believed to be true. But, on reaching the colony again, I found myself to be regarded as rather a bad man, in having come a second time among people whom I had so grossly maligned. No good word that I had said was held in any remembrance; but any hint conveying censure was treasured up and quoted against me with indignation. I was shown an article in a newspaper in which my mendacity, malignity, and general fiendishness were dilated on with all an editor's eloquence. The custom-house officer who passed my luggage heaped coals of fire on my head by allowing my things to pass through without examination, although I had accused the colony of "blowing." He was very courteous, but full of wrath, and I felt the coals of fire. Some little girls whom I had dearly loved bade me welcome warmly, "although I had not said nice things about the Australian girls." Had I sworn that every girl in the colonies was perfect in beauty, manners, intellect, and acquirements, no one would have told my young friends what I had said. I was met everywhere in the same spirit. My old personal friends were kind to me as before, but they generally whispered to me that others were offended with me. Whenever I required courtesy I found it, but I was always conscious that I was expected to feel the coals of fire. Self-praise in the colonies is called "blowing"; and I had unfortunately said to the colonists—"Don't blow." The phrase that had gone so much against the grain with the young man at the custom-house had condemned me altogether.

When a traveller has been fêted, kindly used, and altogether treated well, he would fain not say evil things of those who have been hospitable to him; and when he thinks well also of such a people he will surely find it easy to abstain from offence. One would think so! But, in writing of races as in speaking of individuals, nothing short of absolute unalloyed eulogy will suffice to give satisfaction. In our daily intercourse with one another we do not tell our friends exactly what we think of them. Who would keep a friend if he did so? But, in writing of a people, an author, if he intend to be of service, must speak the truth, and the whole truth, as far as he sees it. And then offence will come. The individual patriot who has been hospitable feels that his hospitality has been betrayed if a syllable be printed which conveys censure of the country which he loves.

Of the success of these Australian colonies, in using general terms, it is almost impossible to speak too highly. An opening for success in life has been given to men and women who could have earned nothing beyond bare subsistence in England, and labour has been remunerated, dignified, and educated. I have sometimes thought that I have never seen demeanour in man more manly, more noble, or more gratifying than that which I have met at the bottom of the shaft of a gold mine. Certainly I have never seen greater plenty than that which prevails round the wool-shed of a squatter at shearing time. And as for education, I have been astonished, and sometimes carried altogether beyond my own limited range, by the erudition of school boys and school girls. But man after all is but man; and the millennium has not been reached as yet. It is not given even to the Australian colonists to be perfect in all things. What, then, shall a poor chronicler do who wishes to represent the truth, and who yet knows that all that he may say in praise will be, to those spoken of, as nothing to the one word of censure? To the ardent, self-satisfied colonist he will be mendacious, malignant, almost fiendish, if he have touched with irreverent hands, or even failed to touch with admiring hands, the one beloved matter! Could the chronicler have his wish, his words would never find their way at all back to the country of which they are written. There they can do little or no good. It is his object to tell what he sees to those at home who have not had an opportunity of seeing. By them he will be credited or discredited, according to the evidence which they may have of his veracity and the opinion they may form of his judgment. With them, at any rate, there will be no feeling of injury done or of kindness ill-requited because the rosy hue of eulogy may sometimes be tinged by the sober grey of admonition, or spotted here and there with a black patch of censure. But the chronicler's words, when printed, will fly about the world, and will be most eagerly read by the very persons for whom they are not intended. This column, gentlemen, will too probably find its way back to some colonial brother of yours, by whom my words will again be submitted to a criticism which will perhaps be more patriotic than just. If it be so, I can only ask that brother editor and his readers to remember that praise undeserved is satire in disguise. I will speak the truth, and have spoken the truth, to the best of my ability. In doing so of Victoria I have found myself happily able to be loud in her praise. And I can continue to speak in that tone. But even Victoria is not a perfect Elysium.

It should be clearly understood by those who wish to think correctly of the British colonies, that they should be regarded chiefly as a new and happier home for the labouring classes. In coming to this conclusion, the student will first have to teach himself what is a colony; in doing which he must not be guided by any official list of British dependencies. A British colony is, I think, a land in which Britons may earn their bread from the soil under the protection of the British Crown. India we do not call a colony; nor is it one in any proper sense, as the English who live there are very few, and are confined to those who rule the real people of the land. Ceylon we do call a colony, guided by certain official traditions; but Ceylon is no more a colony than are the Indies colonies. Nor is Hong Kong a colony, nor, in the proper sense of the word, are the West Indies. The list of the so-called colonies which are not colonies would be a long one, including, of course, Gibraltar, Malta, and Bermuda, held for military purposes; our settlements on the coast of Africa, held for humanitarian purposes; and such spots about the world as Heligoland and the Falkland Islands, held because we happen to have them. But the list of our true colonies would not be long, and would include little beyond Canada and the Australasian group. If to these we add the Cape colonies, I think we shall have named all the places to which an Englishman may go with the hope of improving his condition as a labourer under the British Crown. But this student should of course also bear in mind that the greatest British colony of all is the United States. It is not under the

British Crown, but is not on that account the less open to British enterprise.

It is well to insist upon this, because most of those who talk of the colonies at home, and almost all who in the colonies talk of themselves, are thinking, when they so talk, of the life and interests and well—or ill— being of the moneyed class. And the visitor who goes to a colony and returns, moves only among the moneyed class, and thinks but little of the outside multitude. And this is of course natural. The man with comfortable means of living has time to talk, has time to write and to read, and can afford to employ his mind on speculative questions. But, to the labourer, the one important thing is to get his 6s., or his 8s., or his 10s. a-day. We are very intent on giving the workman his due share of political importance, and some among us have been able to induce him to make use of it in a mild way; but the working man who would prefer 5s. a-day with any amount of political privileges to 7s. 6d. with none has not yet, I think, been discovered. The workman, whom we are taught to regard as irrepressible, and who certainly is so when his wages are in question, is generally content to be silent on other matters. As a natural consequence of this, he hardly holds the importance which is due to him in the consideration of the world at large. Let any one who has talked about Australia, and read about Australia, bethink himself whether his mind has not been chiefly occupied with squatters, master miners, members of parliament, bankers, ambitious tradesmen, place-holders and governors. To these have been added the noble band of Australian explorers, Australia having given peculiar scope for exploring enterprise. He will have heard something of the labourer at his work, and will be glad to know that he is well paid and well fed. And he will have been told of a certain independence about the females as they wait upon their employers, and will perhaps have been told also that this independence is far from pleasant. But he should, I think, permit himself to understand that this good payment and sufficiency of food, and self-asserting independence of manner, are the very results which should be aimed at in the science of colonisation. What man of wealth in England can justify to himself the difference of position which he sees and feels between himself and the poor hedger and ditcher, whose limbs are racked with rheumatism as he works, up to his knees in mud, on an onion and a lump of bread and cheese? The man of wealth does not attempt to justify it, but satisfies his own conscience by telling himself that it is God's doing, and unavoidable. The philanthropist in England feels that the condition of the English hedger and ditcher can be improved only by very slow steps. But if he will travel here, or in Canada, or in the States, or if without travelling he will acquire knowledge about these countries, he will learn that the condition of the man whom at home he is bound to pity, whom he can sometimes hardly regard without doubting the wisdom of the All-Wise, may be raised by very quick steps to a level on which that idea of injustice ceases to afflict him. This is the view of our colonies which the student should take, and this is the idea which he

should wish to see carried out. If this amelioration of
the working man's condition is there being effected—
if the masses of men and women there are flourishing
and in a condition to flourish, he may, I think, pass
over other matters lightly; he may dismiss political
imbroglios from his mind, or regard them with easy indifference; and may look even upon that great question
of loyalty to the mother country as one of second-rate
importance. That question of bread and cheese—or
rather, as it exists in the colonies, of beef and mutton—with all the concomitant comforts which follow
the first great comfort of a sufficient diet, is of such
paramount importance, and has to be answered with
such an agony of remorse in some of the old countries,
that, when the number of those concerned is considered, no other question comes near to it. Of what
account is the wealth of twenty thousand if twenty million be in need? What consolation can a sense of his
country's glory give to a man whose children cry for
bread? To those who have enough, and twice more
than enough, patriotism and the pride of power, and
the enduring honour of a great nationality, are luxuries indeed. With a full stomach and easy limbs, and
a knowledge that nothing is wanting for the morrow,
he may revel in the memories of Blenheim, Trafalgar,
and Waterloo; but, unless a country can feed its people, and educate them, and so treat them that life
shall be a source of enjoyment and not of pain, such
memories are of but small moment. They are, indeed,
spoken of and written of by those who can enjoy
them. They are among the luxuries of the rich; but,

like other luxuries, they are a source almost of pain to him who thinks of the inferiority of the very poor.

We are doing, perhaps, all that can be done at home; but at home it is slow work. Throughout these colonies, and perhaps more especially here in Victoria than elsewhere, the work is being done not slowly. The working man eats and drinks and holds his own, and looks you in the face; and, though he serves you—as one man must always serve another—he is not your slave. If this be so—and I think that no one who has travelled through these provinces will deny it—then the colonies have been a success. And with those who talk about the colonies at home, and write about them, it is, I think, the first duty to declare that such is the case, in order that they who still have within their hands the power of shaping their own destiny may consider how far it may be well for them to place themselves on this soil.

If in the book which I wrote I said this, as I am saying it now—and I claim to assert that I did do so—then I think that in my small way I did the colonies what good service was within my power. Had I gone on to declare that the rapid growth of colonial life had pro-duced that refinement of manner and delicacy of sentiment which centuries give to an old country, and which perhaps are hardly compatible with the more robust and healthy conditions of life, I think that none would have believed me at home, and that some would have despised me in the colonies.

It will be my chief intention in the few further letters which I shall write to you from these colonies, to point out how far the good things of which I have spoken do fall to the lot of the labourer here, and to express an opinion of the class of labourer who would be justified in coming to seek them. For it is not every man who calls himself a labourer, or every woman who thinks that she can serve, who would find prosperity here. While performing this task, it may be that I shall advert again, in passing, to the manners and mode of living of those who pay for this labour and become rich by doing so. I trust that by nothing that I may say will the susceptibilities of any Australian reader be wounded; but should I press heavily on any one, let him remember how greatly I admire the country of his adoption.

Letter IX

ALL THE WORLD knows that Australia has been made what she is very much by her gold mines, and most of the world knows that, of all the Australian colonies, Victoria has hitherto been the most successful in her search after gold. Since July, 1851, the date usually given for the discovery of gold in Victoria, up to the end of 1873, the value of the gold found in the colony has been £173,000,000, amounting to nearly three times the whole revenue collected in the colony during that period. What has been the profit made on that gold by the finders it would be very hard to say. But in thinking of all this gold, the thinker must by no means allow himself to imagine that it has been all profit. The expense of converting the interior of a hillside into gold fit for the manufacture of sovereigns is very great indeed, and sometimes the expense of dragging out the inside of a hill, when no gold is found to repay the miner, is as great. There are those in the colony now who say that all the gold in Australia has been raised at a cost greater than its value. It is certain that very much has been brought to light under these unhappy circumstances.

With reference to the majority of gold mines, it is now known, as in any other enterprise, what is expended and what is received, and what dividend the produce yields on the capital invested. But for a long period no such knowledge could be acquired. Men worked, not in large companies, but in small gangs—washing the gold out of the muddy gullies and small creeks; and no record was taken of the money which they brought with them, or of the labour which they expended. No wages were paid, as they were all masters. Many a well-born wretch from England was tempted out, with what money he could collect in his pocket, who instead of making his fortune died in abject want among the diggers. Who can compute how much such a one threw into the general stock of loss? Who can say how much money was thus expended with absolutely no result in produce? A true report of the expenditure and receipts in this great enterprise can never be furnished. But, whatever may have been the fortune of the individual adventurers, there can be no doubt as to the wealth and benefits which the gold mines have conferred upon the colonies at large. There is an allurement in gold which no dangers can lessen, no sufferings extinguish. There was gold to be got, and men rushed to get it. The first whispers of gold produced a population which no other charm of Australian life could create, and the whispers soon raised themselves into one long shout, which made Victoria the first gem in the colonial crown of the empire. It is still remembered here how men came in crowds from the adjacent colonies; how rapidly they arrived from England and Ireland; from Germany; even from the United States, and from China—before there was shelter to cover them, or even bread for them to eat. Tales are still current in the colony of the almost fabulous prices which were paid for the means of subsistence at the diggings. There were no roads, and £100 a ton was the common price of conveyance for goods over 60 or 70 miles of ground. The digger who would not walk the distance paid £10 to be carried, and the man who had the money paid it willingly, in order that his hands might be in the gullies a day or two the sooner. And we remember in England with what avidity goods were sent out to the new and precious land. A merchant who had aught to dispose of could not send it quickly enough to Melbourne, in order that it might be bought at ten times its ordinary value by men who in the course of a few weeks had been taught to disregard all question of price by the maddening acquisition of pure gold. And thus not only miners came, but also the wiser tribe who condescended to cater for the miners' wants. Houses were built, and banks were opened—and with the banks, schools and churches. And thus a colony was formed, owing its existence almost as much to those who failed as to those who succeeded. Whether it be good or bad to go into the gold trade may be doubted, but there can be no doubt that it is a fine thing to belong to a gold colony.

Many of your readers may remember a yellow and not very beautiful obelisk near the entrance of the second London Exhibition, the dimensions of which professed to show the amount of gold in cubic inches which had been found in Victoria during the ten first years of its production. Perhaps on looking at it then we did not think that the heap would be the means of making a great nation. There can, I think, be no doubt now of the fact. Australia did not grow corn—did not at any rate grow it in such abundance that she could become great, as have done many of the United States, by feeding the world outside. She was not apparently rich in iron, nor had she at that time produced sugar or cotton. Her rivers were not fit for internal traffic, so that there was hardly hope that cities could be built beyond the margin of the sea. Up to that time the country had been used by us as a depôt for our convicts, and it had with us an ill flavour, as having been converted to such a purpose. Its one source of wealth was pastoral—and a pastoral country must of necessity be thinly inhabited, unsocial, and poor in its resources. Let any one picture to himself the difference between the downs of Sussex and the mining valleys of Glamorganshire. Then the gold was found, and Victoria was soon rivalling California. Downs infinitely wider than those of Sussex were riddled with mining claims much more closely packed than those of Glamorganshire. Corn and iron, and those other good things which had hitherto been so keenly desired, became despicable. Gold would be able to do everything! Who would work for paltry wages who could pick up nuggets? Who would tend sheep when happy diggers could find Pactolian gullies, each with its own El Dorado of gold? There was much of confusion, wonderful success, heartrending failure, debasing triumph, and suicidal misery. All the evils which attend both sudden inflation and sudden depression came upon the miners; but the colony was made, and Melbourne grew to be a great city among the nations.

And how is it now? From that day to this there has been no cessation in the search for gold, and no falling off in its production of such a nature as to create discomfiture. In 1853, which was the year of years, over three million ounces were sent out of the colony. That and the produce of the next four years may be said to represent the state of things when the rivers ran gold, when men had but to wash the mud in the gullies to find the wealth on the surface. In the last ten years it has averaged about a million and a-half of ounces, sometimes rising and sometimes falling, partly as fortune may bring the gold to the grist, but partly also as that special industry may for the nonce be more or less popular with the capitalists and with the labourers of the colony. The last year past—1874—has been the worst year as yet known, the produce having fallen as low as 1,012,152 ounces.

But during the 25 years which have now passed since gold was first found in the colony, the whole nature and manner of the trade have been changed. I do not know how far your readers may be aware of the difference between alluvial gold and gold got by the crushing of rock, or of what is here called quartz. At the risk of some ridicule for attempting to teach that which is already well known, I will explain that alluvial gold is, or at any rate may be, got by the easy process of washing dirt, and that is the gold which the freaks of nature have placed in the soft soil; whereas the gold produced by crushing has to be extracted from the solid rock, which is pounded into dust and converted into mud in order that the gold may be extracted from it by chemical appliances. I need hardly say how great must be the difference in the resources needed for the two operations. A pickaxe and a dish may serve for the one, whereas enormous machinery and the expenditure of vast capital are wanted for the other. And, in the first days, a pickaxe and a dish sufficed for alluvial washing, the bigger grains of gold only being caught—while the smaller were returned to the stream, to be found again as gold became scarce, by more patient miners.

But though the pickaxe and the dish—or the cradle, which worked quicker than the dish—did for a while suffice for alluvial gold, it was soon found that mining operations of a heavy kind were necessary also in search of this. The soil which had once been alluvial had by other freaks of nature been carried deep into the bowels of the earth, and might be traced 500 to 750 feet, and no doubt to an infinitely greater depth, below the surface. When it was obtained, washing only, and not crushing, was necessary; but it had to be obtained by the expenditure of capital, and when obtained it had to give its dividend of profit in proportion to that expense. There was something much more jolly in the simple nugget. The happy finder put his £20 or £30 into his waistcoat pocket, and knew nothing of capital or of dividends.

The simple nugget may still be found—if not on old diggings, where I fear it is scarce, yet in some hitherto unknown and unworked gold regions. The prospect of finding it is always present and alluring to some men; but, as a rule, gold mining has settled down into a regular trade in Victoria. It is carried on by capital, and the miners themselves work generally for regular wages. There are the alluvial mines, the greatest of which are to be found in the neighbourhood of Ballarat; and the quartz mines, the grandeur of which may be said chiefly to preside at Sandhurst—which some of us who are old remember under the less alluring name of Bendigo. I did not, on this occasion, visit Ballarat. Three years since I was there, and went down more than one of its mines. I was even then told that, as regarded the production of gold, Ballarat had seen its palmy days. It was an excellently built city, having within itself all the comforts of civilisation which are to be found in our own towns, and some, I must add, which are not always provided by ourselves. But Ballarat, I was then assured, must look forward to a life in great measure independent of its gold, and this verdict I now find to be more general in men's mouths even than then. Sandhurst is keeping up its head, but even at Sandhurst things are not as brilliant as they were three or four years since. This was the general opinion that I heard at Melbourne, and it was not contradicted even at Sandhurst. It must be borne in mind, however, that the prosperity of such places will always vacillate, and that a decrease in the production of two or three years can hardly be taken as any indication that the supply of gold is coming to an end. The gold-bearing quartz has to be traced through the bowels of the earth with infinite difficulty and patience. Such have been the convulsions and reconvulsions of nature that a lode which has evidently flowed in a certain direction and in a liquid state, through some vast open crevice, will suddenly cease, and be found again on a lower level, but running still in the same direction. Then it will vanish, or seem to be at an end, as though the crevice had been open no further to receive the molten matter in which, by other freaks of nature, the gold had been mixed in infinitesimal particles. Further on, but always running in accordance with some laws which are as yet only in course of becoming known, it will be found again. There in a stratum more or less broad will run the auriferous quartz through the useless rock, which in miners' phraseology is called mullock; and this quartz, being separated and dragged out from crevices 500, 750, or sometimes 1000 feet beneath the surface, will yield gold, at so many pennyweights to the ton of quartz. Two or three ounces to the ton have been given under happy circumstances. Three or four pennyweights is not uncommon, but will hardly pay. Six pennyweights will perhaps give fair interest for the money invested. Eight pennyweights and upwards will make glad the hearts of the shareholders. From all this it must be evident that a falling off in the produce of gold may be temporary, and that any sudden increase can hardly be hoped to be permanent.

This quartz, when brought to the surface, is crushed into dust by stampers worked by machinery, and then turned into mud by the infusion of water. I visited two crushing-houses at Sandhurst, in one of which were 48 stampers, and in the other 96. The noise is so incessant and so loud that it is impossible for the visitor to hear a word of the explanation which, in spite of all difficulties, is bellowed into his ears by his good-natured companion. Then from the mud the gold is extracted, chiefly by the use of quicksilver, and the refuse, after various processes adopted to deprive it of its last remaining particles of gold, is restored to the earth, not in a most becoming condition for picturesque purposes. I found, in reference to the mine at Sandhurst which I descended on the present occasion, that it cost, on an average, about 20s. a ton to raise the quartz, and that the present yield of gold per ton of quartz was sold for 31s. But I fear that the mines of Sandhurst generally were not doing as well as that.

In visiting these mines a stranger will be most interested by the physical condition of the men employed. I found that in the Bendigo district, which includes Sandhurst and its suburbs, there is a population of about 50,000, and that among these there are about 9000 working miners. But, as matters are at present, there is not work for the whole of this number. As the claims pay, or cease to pay, the number of men at work is increased or decreased. And at the present moment there is rather a glut of men than of work. A miner, when out of work, will generally search for gold on his own account, and the man who knows what he is about will still make a living. But as twenty years ago men could hardly be got to work for wages, and as ten, and even three years ago, they liked the chance and risk of speculation on their own account, so now do they prefer the more wholesome certainty of regular wages.

At Sandhurst, three years ago, men were earning 10s. a-day for work in the shafts; but, as I have said before, mining was then very lively. At present they are earning 7s. 6d. a-day, for which they do eight hours' work a-day—the men working in three shifts, so that labour is continuous from 12 o'clock on Sunday night to 12—or rather to 11:30—on Saturday night. A miner's wages are therefore £2 5s. a-week. On this he can live with all comfort. For his meat he pays 4d. a pound. Other articles of consumption are about the same price as in England—always excepting beer, of which the Australian miner is not a large consumer. He drinks but very little—unless it be that on some unfortunate occasion he has a bout of drinking. Even this, I was assured at Sandhurst, is now rare. He has generally built a small house for himself, so that he pays no rent, and the State provides him with free education for his children.

A finer-looking set of men, or better mannered, or endowed more thoroughly with the outer signs of manliness, I think it would be difficult to find in any country or at any employment. But it must be remembered that it is not open to every able-bodied labourer to be a miner. He must learn his trade; and I was told that most of those employed at regular wages have learned it from their very youth. Many of them are Cornishmen. Many more have been born in the colonies, but they have generally been the children of miners. It is a business which is specially apt to descend from father to son.

Letter X

In 1871, when the last census was taken, Melbourne, with its suburbs, contained 206,780 inhabitants;[27] and in saying this it is fair to remark at the same time that the suburbs of Melbourne are so completely a part of the town that, except for municipal purposes, there is no division. Montreal—which is, I think, the largest town in our colonial empire outside of Australia—contained in the same year 107,225 souls. I make the contrast that I may the more readily bring home to the reader's mind the amazingly rapid growth of a town which 40 years ago had no existence at all, and which as a city has been but 25 years in growing. In 1836, the whole population of the region, then called Port Phillip District, and now called Victoria, was 177. In 1851, the entire colony had 77,345 inhabitants. Then gold was found, and it is now computed that the numbers are very little short of 800,000. In 1872 they amounted to 765,240. Your readers are of course aware that Victoria is only one out of six Australian colonies. The others are New South Wales, the parent of them all; Tasmania, and Queensland, which were divided off from New South Wales, as was also Victoria; and Western Australia and South Australia, which started for themselves. To these, to make up the Australasian group, must be added the thriving provinces of New

---

[27] In 1933 the population of Melbourne was 991,934.

Zealand; and now I suppose the new colony which we call Fiji, and which certainly has not as yet begun to thrive. When we think of our three millions of persons in London, and of the 40 millions in the United States—for our American cousins boast that they have now reached that number—the population of Victoria and of Melbourne does not much strike us; but when the time is considered, and the outward circumstances, which in Australia did not at first offer many advantages to great numbers, the progress must be acknowledged to have been very great. As I said in my last letter, Australia—or New Holland as it was then called—was first used by us as a receptacle for convicts. The Dutch had found the land—and, indeed, the Portuguese before the Dutch, if the records be true. But Dutch explorers had followed one another in quick succession, and have left their names on various parts of the continent. And a Frenchman was there before any Englishman had come. But neither Portuguese nor Dutch, neither French nor English, had done anything towards the occupation of the land, till Captain Cook reached it in 1770. It was in compliance with his counsel that the British Government determined to claim possession of the vast region, and by his advice that Commodore Phillip was sent with a band of convicts to Botany Bay in 1787. That was the first occupation of Australia by any civilised people, and it was one neither adapted nor intended to give rise to a popular colony.

In writing to you from Sydney, I may revert to the convict establishment there, and to the heroism displayed by the British governor in the terrible task of looking after his refractory subjects. I allude to the matter now only to show how little the commencement of our career in Australia could do to promise national or colonial greatness. Then, as by degrees they who had been sent out to feed and to control the convicts settled in the country, and as the convicts by degrees worked their way to complete or to comparative freedom, they looked about them for some mode of making money in the new land; and when, with infinite difficulty—with difficulties from thick woods, and rocky mountains, and angered savages—they had made their way up from the seaboard into the interior, they found that there were wide pastures on which flocks might be fed. Sheep were introduced, and the growth of wool became the staple commerce of the country. But pastoral pursuits are by no means conducive to large population or the growth of cities. When it takes three acres to feed a sheep, men cannot congregate closely together while feeding them. For many years, up indeed to 1851, the growth of wool was the one great enterprise for which Australia was known. Our Australian empire had thus become important to us as a land to which we could banish some of our ruffians, and from which we could get some of our wool. Neither on the one hand nor on the other was it likely to become a great country. Up to 1851 we thought very little about the country at home, except that we had already been made to understand that the old colonies which had been so serviceable to us in regard to our transportation would take no more convicts. The population, though still sparse, were sufficient to find that they could now live better by their own labour than with the assistance of labour tainted by crime. But still up to 1851 the prospect before them was not very bright. A race of squatters had arisen, who were making money—some of whom were already making large fortunes. Of these, the aristocrats of the colony, I shall say something in writing to you from New South Wales. But outside the squatting interest, beyond the growth of wool, there was little or nothing to give importance to Australia. Then gold was found! It was discovered in Victoria and New South Wales almost exactly at the same time, but in much greater plenty in Victoria. This was in 1851; and since that time have sprung up a people second to none in their own opinion, strong in energy, strong in industry; battling and grasping, making speeches and editing newspapers, governing themselves with more than the ordinary bustle of parliament and responsible ministers; often ignorant, always conceited, abusive among each other with more than British violence, but determined to succeed, determined to grow and to become rich—and succeeding, growing, and becoming rich accordingly.

In this way Melbourne has become a great town, by far the greatest congregation of British human beings outside the British Isles. It will be observed that it contains above a quarter of the population of the entire colony—a population which is excessive, and, as far as the evidence goes, tells badly for the agricultural interests. Men prefer to live where they can be engaged in manipulating the production of others rather than in producing themselves. Consequently, though large districts of Victoria are capable of growing wheat, she is driven to import grain. But there they are, these 200,000 human beings, eating and drinking and enjoying life. Very little poverty meets the eye. Three years ago I saw no street beggars. On the present occasion one or two have asked me for money, but even these have had about them a look of colonial well-being. Artisans in Melbourne, such as masons, bricklayers, and carpenters, now earn from 8s. to 10s. a-day. Twenty years ago they were earning from 20s. to 30s. But 20 years ago everything in Melbourne was so dear that the man's condition was hardly better than it is now. Men-servants, such as grooms and gardeners, are earning from £40 to £50 per annum, with board and lodging. A plain cook receives from £30 to £40—other maid-servants from £25 to £35 per annum. Farm labourers through the colony are paid from 15s. to 20s. a-week, with their rations. A shepherd, whose work is supposed to be the lowest class of work, gets from £25 to £35 per annum, with rations. In shearing time, the shearers of sheep will earn from 12s. to 15s. a hundred; and as he will shear, on an average, 350 sheep a-week, he will receive from something under 40s. to something over 50s. a-week. But shearing is skilled labour; it lasts but from ten to twelve weeks in the year; and the shearer finds his own provisions. The value of money wages is, however, only relative, and depends on the cost of provisions. In Melbourne, butchers' meat ranges from 3d.

to 7d. per lb. In country towns it is cheaper—say from 2d. to 5d. Bread is nearly the same as in England, the difference, if there be a difference, being in favour of the colony. Clothes, upon which protective duties are levied, are somewhat dearer in Victoria than at home. Fuel, if purchased, is dearer in the towns, coals running in Melbourne from 30s. to 35s. a ton; but the climate requires but little fire, and in the country wood is cheap. Rent in the towns is dearer than in England, but the labourer's facility of building for himself or living without rent is greater. Upon the whole a labourer's money will, I think, go further in Victoria than in England—though a gentleman's money will not go so far. The labourer is ministered to by himself or his wife. He who wants other ministers has to pay dearly for them. Nor is the labourer troubled by school fees. The education of his children is supplied free by the State, and is very good. Whether too much be not taught, and technical aids to education be not too often relied on, so as to produce what school pundits call results, is a question into which I need not enter now. The fault, if there be such fault, is to be found also in England and in the United States. The collected wisdom of the school pundits has not, probably, as yet found out the best mode of educating the children either of the rich or poor. But the work-man in Victoria will certainly think that the Victorian Government has found out the best mode of paying the schoolmaster.

Political privileges the working man also has in Victoria—if he desires them. Universal manhood suffrage prevails; and the man, whether he be a householder, a lodger, or only simply a man, can vote for a member of the Legislative Assembly. As political power in the colony depends on a majority of votes in the assembly—just as with us it does on a majority in the House of Commons—the working man is much courted. The working men of Victoria, no doubt, elect the assembly, and can, therefore, dictate their own measures. But here, as elsewhere, the working man, of himself, does not care much for politics, and allows certain busybodies to dictate to him the measures which he is supposed to dictate to others. The busybodies lately have not, I think, been very wise, as they have induced the voters to demand protection—the natural consequence of which has been the enforced use of ill-made articles and enforced abstinence from many comforts.

The working man has another advantage in all these colonies, which is apparent to me at every step I take and in every man I look at, but which I find it very difficult to explain in language that shall not appear to be more democratic than my opinions. But if I say that the hat-touching aspect of the working man, with its too usual concomitants of displayed servility and concealed hostility, has not cropped up here, your readers will perhaps understand me. The hat-touching aspect has its charms. When the model labourer at home uncovers his head to the model landlord, regarding the benign big man almost as a special parochial providence, and the big man accepts the homage with an inward acknowledgment that by doing so he binds himself to various duties on behalf of his worshipper, the whole thing is very pretty, and to the feminine mind seems to be almost perfect. I complain of it chiefly because the worship is generally false, and the worshipped one so seldom worthy of it. Whether it be good or ill, it does not exist here. The man who takes wages does not at all feel himself bound to lift his hat to the man who pays him, or to acknowledge his inferiority by any outward sign. But in lieu of such submissiveness there has grown up a manly demeanour, combined with an open smiling courtesy, which to me leaves very little to be desired in manner.

Such is the condition of the Victorian labourer as I have found it, and the picture is one which I think ought to be attractive to the working man at home. But there is the reverse side of it, at which he should look very carefully, and which he will find it much more difficult to examine and digest, and take home to himself, than that which will have charmed him. He must ask himself in the first place whether he can be sure of his own sobriety. Beer may be a snare to him at home, and, if so, will do him much damage. But, if it be so, bad brandy and bad whisky will certainly kill him in the colonies. When men do drink here, they drink to terrible excess. He must then ask himself whether he can really work. Of course he thinks that he can; but he may perhaps be able to ascertain, by some course of self-examination, whether he is good among his fellow-workmen, or whether he be slow and unhandy. It is the handy man who does well here—the man who has a head on his shoulders, and a quick touch, and a sharp eye. Of course it may be said that a man with such qualities will do well anywhere. At home the man without them has to do, or in some shape to be done for; but he at any rate had better not emigrate. Then, again, it should be remembered, in considering these things, that a young man may, by certain incentives, be induced to learn to be handy. Unless he be by nature specially dull he will acquire the ways and manners of those around him, and fit himself for the duties demanded from him. The man who has passed into middle life, and has hardened himself into certain habits of life, cannot do this. Therefore it is the young man who should emigrate. And this young man must remember that, in return for high wages and ample diet, hard work will be required of him. In the towns a rule is becoming gradually universal by which this work is restricted to eight hours a day; but during those eight hours he must really work. In the country, no such arrangement is possible. There is much of task work, such as shearing, the making of fences, and clearing of timber, at which, for his own sake, he will make long hours. And there will be other work on farms, or among sheep and cattle, at which fixed times will be impossible. But, whatever be his employment, while he is at it he must work. I should have told him of what his food will consist if he be employed in country districts, which food, under the name of rations, will be supplied to him in addition to his wages. He will have of meat allowed to him 14 lb. a-week, of flour 10 lb., of sugar 2 lb., and of tea ¼ lb. There may be some slight variations in different localities; but as a rule these will be the provisions afforded to him, and these he will be required to cook for himself. Should he want further dainties he must pay for them. But the dietary is one which the ordinary English rural labourer may, I think, regard without dismay. One thing more must be added. No beer will be allowed him, nor for long periods will he even see or hear of beer. He will have to accustom himself to long periods of work, during which he will bind himself not to drink intoxicating liquors. This, of course, refers to country labour. If, after these periods, he can still refrain, it will not be long before he finds himself the owner of freehold land. His wages will come to him in large sums—his entire wages for three months, probably, at the same time—and then, if he can keep himself from revelling, he will have nothing to do with it but to invest it.

But there is one class of workmen, or of intending workmen, who should never come to the colony. This is the young gentleman, who, finding that nobody wants him at home, thinks that he may as well emigrate. Neither will any one want him here. And here no one will pity him. At home he may get some compassion and some aid.

Letter XI

ON MY ARRIVAL HERE, at the beautiful city of Sydney, the capital of New South Wales—the spot at which we first attempted to use our possession of New Holland, as Australia was then called—I found all the world agog on an expedition about to be made by Mr. William Mackay to the neighbouring island of New Guinea, with the object of investigating the mysteries of that altogether unknown country. If any of your readers will think of it, I doubt whether they will not find that they know less about New Guinea or Papua than any other inhabited portion of the earth's surface. The island has been visited, but no more than visited. There is no European or white man living on it—not even a missionary. Its latitude and longitude are of course known, and its coast line is marked on our maps with more or less accuracy. Its size and position in seas that are now open to commerce have made so much a necessity. Lying as it does, not amidst Arctic or Antarctic ice, but immediately south of the line, within 100 miles of Australia, and running a length of more than 1200 miles from the Spice Islands on the west towards the Solomon Islands on the east, it occupies too central a position in the world to have escaped the notice of the surveyors and mapmakers; but of its interior we have learned infinitely less than of the interior of Africa, Australia, or British North America.

No serious attempts at investigation have yet been made, and yet it is, or is said to be, the largest island in the world—always excepting Australia, which the geographers now call a continent. Borneo, which is cut by the line, has been made known to us by the enterprise of Rajah Brooke, and a portion of it has, I fear, been entailed upon us as a future colony. Java has for many years been in the possession of the Dutch. Ceylon belongs to us, and is thoroughly prosperous. The Mauritius enjoys more or less of prosperity under the same rule. Of New Zealand, with its wealth, its ambition, and its financial troubles, I need hardly speak. New Caledonia has become a French Botany Bay. The group of islands which we now call Fiji, and which I hope to visit before I reach home, we have—I am afraid, unfortunately—already annexed. Of the Sandwich Islands, with their kings and queens, we know as much as, or almost more than, we do of Ireland. But New Guinea is still a closed book to us. There are men there whom we know to be savages, whom we believe to be cannibals, who have never yet had guns or gunpowder introduced to their notice. We have never traded with them, as we did from Cook's time down with the New Zealanders. These men are black, as the Australian aborigines, not brown like the Maoris. Travellers who have touched the coast have brought us word that their ignorance is extreme and their habits abominable. Rumour has said that they carry gold ornaments; but great doubt has been thrown upon what rumour has said in this respect. Pearls have certainly been found on the southern coast. Of its animal and vegetable life we are at present entirely ignorant. It is primarily with the object of getting information on this latter subject—of investigating what are now generally called the fauna and flora of the country, that Mr. Mackay is making his expedition.

Immediately on my arrival in Sydney, I heard that he was to start on the following day, and a card was sent to me asking me to join a party which was to go down with him to Port Jackson Heads, and there to bid him adieu. The ministry of the day, with that wonderful veteran, Mr. John Robertson, at their head, were to take Mr. Mackay and his companion, Captain Onslow, down in a steamer; then there was to be a banquet, the usual eulogistic speeches, and all the tenderness of a public farewell. As I had previously had the good fortune to be acquainted with these gentlemen, and as Sydney harbour is a spot beaten by none other that I have ever seen in picturesque beauty, and as the day was fine and the air delicious, requiring no greatcoat, and yet being never hot, very little persuasion was wanted to induce me to accept the invitation. Nothing could have been nicer than the little preliminary expedition. The banquet was eaten, and the toasts were drunk, and the speeches were made, and the band played merrily all the time. Then came the farewell, and our two heroes departed into their own vessel, and were tugged out to sea.

Though the whole matter was very interesting, I do not know that I should have endeavoured to pass that interest on to readers in England were it not that a peculiar—and I think a false—importance is attached to the expedition, and that in reference to a subject with which our Colonial Office at home is much exercised at the present moment. The Australian colonies have, no doubt, been greatly gratified by the annexation of Fiji, and especially New South Wales, which, of all the colonies, has been most concerned in the matter. Now, there is growing up an idea that, as the English Government was so easily persuaded to plant a new colony at Fiji, the annexation of New Guinea may be as readily accomplished. Before this letter—which must, of course, take its turn—can have appeared in your columns, Mr. Mackay himself may have returned, and shortly afterwards the results of his labours will be known. But one result will almost certainly be a demand from an influential class in this colony, and from Queensland also, that New Guinea shall be made a new colony. To Mr. Mackay this will almost be unfair. He is undertaking his voyage for scientific purposes, and is doing so in a manner which makes it impossible to speak too highly of his liberality and spirit. He is a man of wealth, and will bear the entire expense himself. This will certainly not be less than £10,000. He will incur much danger, and will undergo considerable privation. A residence among savages can never of itself be pleasant. A residence close under the line is seldom so; nor is the charm increased by the necessity of being constantly on the sea-coast or in the mouths of rivers. It is not the kind of amusement which wealthy men in middle life generally select for themselves. Explorers usually expect at any rate to have their expenses paid, and are hardly satisfied—probably are seldom able—to confer upon their country the results of their labours altogether at their own cost. This is what Mr. Mackay is doing; and there can be but little doubt that his researches, and those of Captain Onslow, will add materially to our present stock of knowledge. It is his purpose to make his way up the Papuan rivers in a launch constructed for the purpose, in which he hopes to make himself safe from the arrows of the natives by means of netting; and if he succeeds in doing this and in returning, we shall then know something of the interior of New Guinea. He and his party will, of course, have fire-arms, and fire-arms are at present unknown there. The result of such expeditions has been almost always the same. A white man or two may be "murdered" in their determination to make themselves masters of the new land; but the savage will succumb, and be driven back—will be coaxed with red cloth and beads—will be perplexed beyond the extent of his poor intellect; and may think himself very lucky if he be not at last brought into the pale of civilisation and quickly polished off the face of the earth as beatified subjects of the British Crown. I do not say that this is Mr. Mackay's intention; it certainly was not his primary idea; and if any such ambition be now within his view, it has probably been thrust upon him by the views of others. To him we are and shall be undoubtedly under a debt of gratitude; but that idea of annexation should, I think, receive very little encouragement in reference to New Guinea.

Men who are at the same time politicians and philanthropists—or who, in other words, concern themselves with the welfare of their own country and of the world at large—find an almost invincible difficulty in the colonisation of new lands. That the teeming populations of old civilised countries should find new fields for their labours in the fertile lands about the world—lands which, when found by them, are populated only in the sparsest manner—seems to be not only expedient but absolutely necessary for carrying on God's purposes with the earth. It is impossible to regret that North America and Australia and South Africa have been opened to British enterprise and British life; and yet we have to acknowledge to ourselves that in occupying these lands we commit a terrible injustice. Though we have struggled against the injustice, it always comes. We have endeavoured to console ourselves by thinking that the peoples would at any rate have become Christians before they had utterly perished. I will not here go into that very vexed question of the possible Christianising of the savage races. But experience seems at any rate to show that the extermination always comes before the Christianity has been realised. The land becomes ours with its fatness—and the people disappear. They cannot endure contact with us—even when, as in New Zealand, we make the most determined struggle to be just. They cannot endure contact with us—even when, as in New Zealand, they are endowed with gifts of intellect and courage much higher than those generally found among savage tribes. It is terrible to think of this extermination. The Maoris are going. The blacks of Tasmania have perished to the last man. The aborigines of Australia are perishing in part, and are partly being driven into the barren interior of their own country. All which seemed to be theirs by as good a title as that which gives any English gentleman his land has been taken from them, for the most part ruthlessly. When they have attempted to oppose us, no names have been too black for their ingratitude, no punishments too severe for their treachery.

But we reconcile ourselves to all this by the necessity of the case, and by the manifest general improvement effected on the world's surface. Thousands live where only tens lived before, and those thousands live in intellectual comfort. The earth which bore nothing is made subject to the plough. Flocks and herds are multiplied, and the seas are covered with ships. The poor wretch who has perished was an abject, idle, useless creature, hideous to our eyes, a cannibal perhaps, low in intellect, and incapable of being taught. Where the wretch was, a dozen men and women, beautiful to look at, are bringing up their children in the fear of the Lord. With this, perhaps slightly exaggerated, estimate of our glories, we keep down our remorse, and the world is peopled. We English are the race to whom this duty, if it be a duty, seems to have been confided; and so we have gone on, annexing one country after another, and have built up our immense colonial empire, having also built up another empire which after a while refused to be colonial any longer.

But how shall we reconcile ourselves to a continua-

tion of this condition of things, to prolonged annexation, if we take from the present possessors lands in
which European men and women cannot live and be
beautiful, or bring up their children at all? Such is
certainly the case with New Guinea. Let any one look
at a map of the world, and follow the line of the equator all round, and see what is being done in those
regions which lie within ten degrees of it, north and
south. Englishmen have lived as taskmasters to others,
but have never lived as workmen. Even India, of
which we are so proud—India, to which we allude
when we speak of those many millions over which our
Queen is sovereign—has afforded no home to our
growing multitudes. All India does not contain as
many Europeans—putting aside the army—as the
little fading island of Tasmania. Ceylon prospers, and
prospers under English rule; but she prospers because
her own race are industrious, and not savage. It surely
cannot be worth our while to annex New Guinea, in
order that a few merchants may be enabled to live—
or die—upon its shores.

The missionary would fain go there, in order that
new tribes may be added to Christ's flock; but he has
many lands already annexed, already open to his enthusiastic piety, if he can Christianise the savage.
Judging from past results, we are justified in saying
that it cannot be worth our while to annex such a
country for religious purposes. Close contact with the
Papuans we could not have—nothing but absolute
occupation of the land will give that; and when our
contact has been close—close, and secure, and benefi-

cent, as in India—even then the labours of our missionaries are not very successful.

But there may be gold in New Guinea, as there certainly is gold on the York Peninsula—that northern jutting-out extremity of Australia which nearly meets the Papuan coast. But if gold there were as certain as it is now doubtful, there would not be in that fact any reason why we should hamper ourselves with the possession of a country which, when the fact was known, would become the resort of Chinese and Malays, who would live and work there; and of some wretched Europeans, who would try to work there and would die. It is already becoming a question whether European miners can live and work for gold on the York Peninsula; but we know enough of the condition of the tropics to be sure that they could not do so in New Guinea.

But the grand argument for annexation of the island, put forward here in the colony, is its proximity to Australia. There are islands, lying off Cape York, which are supposed to belong to us, and are said to be not more than thirty miles from the coast of New Guinea; would it not be sorely detrimental to the honour of Great Britain if any other nationality should occupy a great island so near to our confines? Why it should be detrimental either to our honour or our prosperity I have not had explained to me. If the Dutch should please to make themselves masters of the land, I do not think that their vicinity would be very injurious to us. But we may be tolerably certain that a land with so few allurements will not charm the

Dutch or any other people. There is almost all Borneo for them if they wish to extend their possessions in these latitudes. But neither the Dutch nor any other people will come. If the ungrateful task be forced on any nation, Great Britain will be the sufferer.

In annexing Fiji, which we have done mainly in the interests of the Australian colonies—or in the future annexation of New Guinea, should we be so unfortunate as to be driven into such a step—the colonies would not help us in the expense. New South Wales declined to do so in reference to Fiji, and was, I think, right. A young colony should hardly subject herself to such a burden for speculative advantages. But there can be no reason why England should bear the burden. As regards Fiji, I hope to be able to say a few words in the course of these letters. That work, however, if not exactly done, has at any rate been undertaken, and must now be carried through as best we may. There was at any rate the excuse of a British population, which had become strong enough to domineer over the savagery of the islands, and the Fijians had become accustomed to British ways. No Europeans have as yet been driven to the shores of Papua in the quest of fortune. As some English statesman said, we have surely black subjects more than enough. For Mr. Mackay and his companions I feel great admiration, and with his object great sympathy. But I do hope that we shall not be driven to send a governor with all his staff to New Guinea because it lies near an extreme point of the Australian coast.

Letter XII

SYDNEY, to the ordinary traveller who generally forms his judgment from his eye, is a much more prepossessing city than Melbourne. This sentence, should it ever reach Melbourne, will subject me to heavy censure, as the jealousy between the towns, as between the two colonies of which they are the capitals, is very great; but no stranger who has seen both will doubt the truth of the assertion. The country in which Melbourne stands is not of itself picturesque. It is too far from the sea to be made beautiful by coast scenery. Hobson's Bay, on which its port is situated, is not of itself pretty, nor is Port Phillip, of which Hobson's Bay is a portion, at all lovely to the eye. Melbourne is nobly built, with broad straight streets like an American city, and contains very many handsome buildings. But its river, the Yarra, is insignificant, and its public parks and gardens, though excellent in a sanitary point of view, and perhaps equally so in regard to science, have very little to charm. But Sydney is a paradise of scenic beauty. Port Jackson, the large land-locked harbour on which it stands, is broken into an infinite number of coves, which again subdivide themselves into little rocky bays. These are so numerous that within five miles of the city there is an intricacy of coast scenery which delightfully puzzles the lover of nature who endeavours to map them in his mind. The trees grow down to the very margin of the water, and the water is on every side so cut into small spaces as never to produce the comparative ugliness of a wide expanse. Within a mile—within half a mile—of the centre of the city, all the charm of coast scenery may be found. The governor's house is but five minutes' walk from the Parliament Chambers, and just below the governor's garden, and attached to them, there is a private bathing house among the rocks. I have seen the bays of Dublin and Naples, and the harbour of New York, all celebrated for their beauty; but to my eyes Sydney is more lovely than them all. A man cannot live on scenery, nor live by means of rocky inlets; but if there be the means of living, I think that these things add a great charm to life.

The public gardens of Sydney, which are by no means large, have a peculiar grace of their own, because they possess one of these little coves as their own. The most has been made of these grounds by Mr. Moore, the gentleman in charge of them, and I cannot imagine a more delightful spot for the recreation of a city. The delight, however, is perhaps chiefly in this— that they are close to the town. It is very much to be able to get out of a crowded street into fairy-land in ten minutes and at no expense.

But Sydney, though it has the advantages which picturesque belongings can give it, was not a well-chosen site for the cradle of a new colony, and in its struggle for existence had to endure a world of evils from which Melbourne in its infancy was free. The land around it is very poor, so poor that it produces little or nothing—and the very first requisite for a young people is a fertile soil. When Port Jackson was chosen for the convict settlement, this necessity certainly was not obtained.

In 1770 and 1777, Cook visited the eastern coast of New Holland, and in his reports home recommended the government of the day to establish a convict depôt at a spot which was called Botany Bay, from the luxuriance of its shrubs and flowers. Cook's advice was taken, and in 1787 Commodore Phillip[28] arrived at Botany Bay with his convicts and officers and gaolers—an unhappy enterprise, we may say, for a naval hero. But at the place selected there was no water, and, in spite of the flowers and shrubs, no fertile soil. The commodore, therefore, moved some few miles up the coast, and, entering the spacious harbour which is now called Port Jackson—so named, as report goes, from the sailor who first espied the opening—settled himself and his men on the spot which is now called Sydney.

I know no story proclaiming greater heroism, more heartrending misfortunes, or narrower risks, than that of Commodore Phillip with his convict band. He was one of the world's heroes of whom the world hears little—a stubborn, just, self-denying, long-suffering, brave man, who, when despair was all around him, could work on and do his duty, as other men can do it when success is all but certain. In every emergency, all depended on him. He was not only governor over

[28] Arthur Phillip (1738–1814). To him Australia owes her very existence.

his subjects, but had the life of every man in his own hands. And his subjects required ruling with a very strong hand. A crew of convicts, so far from home, not unnaturally thought, when called upon to work, that rebellion would be easy and absolute emancipation far from improbable. It was necessary that they should work, and there is nothing so odious to such men as daily labour. Food became very scarce. The earth would give them next to nothing; for everything they had to trust to ships from England or from India; and it often seemed to them that they had been forgotten by their absent friends. Every now and then, both convicts and governors were reduced to half rations, with the knowledge—at any rate, on the part of the governor—that the continuance of that modicum depended on the arrival of some long-expected vessel from home. And then, though the country produced nothing, it was by no means uninhabited. Had it been so, half the commodore's troubles would have been spared him. There were the aborigines, of whom Cook, in giving his advice, had spoken, indeed, but certainly had not regarded as owners of the soil. These were a race of men perhaps as low as any that have as yet been found on the earth's surface—black, naked, not living in houses, possessing no individual property, and cannibals; but still owning the land in tribes, and showing their appreciation of ownership by their intertribal jealousies and wars. Then arose that terribly difficult question between justice and the necessity of self-assertion. It certainly never occurred to Governor Phillip that he should abandon the land which he had been directed to occupy, because it was already in the possession of another people. Nor to those who ruled at home had the idea yet come home that justice forbade the English nation to possess itself of a country inhabited, but untilled, by a savage race. We had never colonised then as we have since done in New Zealand, and are now intending to do in Fiji. But still there was a strong feeling in the bosom of Commodore Phillip that he should so use the land as to do good, rather than harm, to those who had hitherto possessed it. If only these poor ignorant creatures could be made to see that he would fain be beneficent to them, all might be well as far as they were concerned. But it is not easy to make a wretched savage understand that you intend to do good to him, when he clearly does perceive that you intend to take away from him everything that he calls his own. The kindly feelings of the commodore were thrown away, and there was superadded to his other difficulties the necessity of internecine war, which it might be necessary to carry on even to extermination.

Among such difficulties as these the colony was formed, but was regarded for many years as being useful only as a place to which we might export our convicted ruffians. But gradually they who had the care of the ruffians, with their growing children, and the friends and servants who followed them out—with the aid also of reformed or enfranchised ruffians—spread themselves abroad, and used the land for more salutary purposes. The skirt of country on which the young Sydney was being built was a strip lying along the seashore, but cut off from the interior by a ridge of mountains, high, rocky, and enveloped in thick timber, which the earliest explorers found it impossible to pass. They were bound in upon the inhospitable shore, with the conviction that if they could but pass that barrier a land flowing with milk and honey would be open to them. With great efforts and many perils the barrier was at length passed, and a vast territory was reached—not flowing, indeed, with milk and honey, not gifted with exceptional fertility, but capable of bearing sheep and cattle, capable in some parts of producing corn, and having in its bosom—though the secret was to be concealed yet for nearly half a century—river courses and rocks laden with gold.

The earliest success of the new colony came from the growth of wool. Captain Macarthur, an officer who had come out with a military corps supposed to be necessary for the suppression of the convicts, had introduced merino sheep, and it had been found possible to make money by them even within the barrier; but the flocks spread, and there came a drought, and then it was that they who owned the flocks were driven to seek for other pastures. When once the Blue Mountains were passed, the capability of the country for the growth of wool seemed to be unlimited, and for our present purposes it is unlimited. It was as a wool-growing country that New South Wales first became a colony, properly so called, instead of a convict settlement, and it is as a wool-growing country that Australia will become a great nation. The value of the gold is consumed as the gold is produced; it leaves little behind it except the population which has come to seek it. But wool creates permanent wealth. The rich aristocracy of Australia—for she has a rich aristocracy—has amassed its possessions chiefly by the growth of wool.

But, before the mountains had been passed, and while yet the absorption of convicts was the benefit which the mother country expected from her distant child, other steps had been taken for the extension of the empire. The country round Sydney having become crowded with convicts, a portion of them were removed to Norfolk Island; but Norfolk Island was distant and inconvenient, and Van Diemen's Land, which lies close to the southern coast of the Australian continent, was found to be preferable. In 1805, a second convict depôt was opened there, and flourished, so far as a convict depôt can be said to flourish. Those among us who are no longer young remember that Botany Bay and Van Diemen's Land were the names which in our youth we associated with expatriated rascaldom. Botany Bay was never used. I do not know that any convict ever set his foot there. Van Diemen's Land has been made sweet as a rose by changing her hated name to Tasmania, the land having been originally discovered by Tasman, who was one among the great sailors of the world, and who, at the time of his discovery, was in love with the daughter of Van Diemen—the father-in-law's name might otherwise never have come to our knowledge. And other convict establishments were made or attempted. One was sent south to the region which we now call Victoria, but did not thrive, finding no water or other necessaries of life. Another was settled at King George's Sound, within the present confines of Western Australia, from whence it was expelled by the stern morals of the Swan River colonists, before they were driven in their need to ask that their fading strength might be recruited by convicts direct from home. And yet another was established at Moreton Bay, which is now called Queensland. And the Queenslanders, though they were resolute in refusing to have a single felon sent to them after their separation from New South Wales, are to the present day much indebted to the labours which convicts performed for them.

Thus the colonies were formed. In 1825 Van Diemen's Land was, at its own request, separated from New South Wales, and started with a governor and responsibilities of its own, though still existing as a convict settlement. In 1836 the district then called Port Phillip, now known all over the world as Victoria, had become sparsely peopled—chiefly by immigrants from Van Diemen's Land—and was first graced with a semi-governor, being still a dependency under New South Wales. In 1851 she was altogether separated from the parent colony. In the same year, gold was first found in Australia—first in New South Wales, and within a month or two in Victoria; but the Victorian diggings were by far the richer, and Victoria at once took the lead among the Australian colonies. Then, in 1839, New Zealand became a dependency under New South Wales; but that arrangement was not lasting, and in 1840 New Zealand received a governor of her own. Since that day we hardly reckon her among the Australian group. In 1859, Moreton Bay having become impatient of her dependency to New South Wales, complaining of the distance to which she was forced to send her few representatives—for at this time parliamentary government had been established—and ambitious of greater independence and increased responsibility, was allowed to proclaim herself as a new colony under the name of Queensland. As Victoria was divided off to the south, so was Queensland to the north. The people to the north of this northern section are already clamouring for further separation, and ultimately, no doubt, their prayer will be granted. Thus four separate colonies were formed out of that of which Sydney with its convicts was the original nucleus. Of Western Australia, which is so far removed from the others as hardly to be in unison with them, I have already spoken. There remains only South Australia, the one of those colonies which has never had a convict on her shores, as she is the only one to which New South Wales has never sent an offshoot. Of her, too, I hope that I may be able to say a word before I have completed these letters.

But, while these separations were being effected, the colonies, having grown in population and wealth, gradually repudiated the purpose for which they had been originally established. When the free element became strong it remonstrated against the continued reception of English felons.

The mother country, of course, yielded. Gradually our statesmen had learned to feel that these emigrant populations must be allowed to manage their own affairs for their own benefit, and not for the sake of us who remained at home; and they had been taught also that in this way could new and happy homes be best found for her overflowing children. Here, in Sydney, the taint of felony has now almost died out. As regards the labour of the colony, I may say that it is not felt at all. Instead of feeling that this or that man has probably left the old country as a convict, one is occasionally startled, and perhaps rather gratified than otherwise, by seeing some veteran who is pointed out as having been not so steady in his youth as he might have been; and old shepherds will sometimes tell tales of their own forcible expatriation, always explaining that in their peculiar case the exercise of some virtue, which had been unhappily twisted out of its proper direction, had led to their misfortune. As regards New South Wales, it should be explained that this happy state of things was much accelerated by her sending to Tasmania the remnant of her convicts when she herself became a free colony. In Tasmania there is still a convict establishment, in which is kept the remaining remnant; and there the taint remains, and will remain till the remnant has altogether died out.

Sydney is now a flourishing old town—a town almost with ruins, and on this account very different from any other place in Australia.[29] It has churches which remind one of the days of George III., and which in London would be rebuilt or remodelled because of their

---

[29] Sydney is now the largest city in Australia, with a 1933 population of 1,235,267.

antiquity. It has its Parliament with its Upper and Lower Houses, its pleasant clubs, its wharves and immense stores, and shops almost as gorgeous as those of the old country. When Commodore Phillip had to rack his brain and calculate how he might best keep his wretched crew alive, he could have little thought that in less than a century such a city would stand on the site of all his troubles.

Letter XIII

I SAID in my last letter that New South Wales had first been made a colony by the growth of wool, and that Australia would become a great nation as a wool-growing country. No doubt the export of gold for the last 22 years has much exceeded the export of wool; and as, both in regard to wool and gold, almost all that is produced is exported, it might appear that the relative value of the one and the other would give an accurate idea of their relative importance. But very little of the gold is brought into the market at a cost of less than two-thirds of its value, while much of it has cost much more than it was worth. It has been far otherwise with wool. The sheep breed and multiply above ground, and feed themselves on wide pastures, which cost but little. The result has been that there are in the colonies breeders of sheep—squatters as they are called—of immense wealth, and a whole class of men who have amassed considerable fortunes by pastoral pursuits; so much so that the Australian squatter is, in all the colonies, felt to be the magnate of the land. He is, above others, the colonial gentleman and aristocrat. He fills the place which is occupied in England by the country gentleman. But, on the other hand, the man who has made his money by gold, and has kept it, is far to seek. They who have been once lucky have been twice unlucky. And there is something in the very nature of gold when thus found which almost justifies the poet who declared that it was best placed when hidden from mortal sight. It unsettles and demoralises the finder, and dissipates itself. The money that comes in from wool sticks to the producer. He is tempted to buy land, which is of all possessions the most alluring. In this way the squatters have become the very backbone of the Australian colonies. There can, I think, be little doubt which is the most picturesque of the two employments. The miner himself, as I have said before, is a fine fellow—pleasant in his manners, and manly in his conduct. But all his surroundings are ugly, I might say hideous. He has company, which the shepherd generally lacks; but he works underground, and when he comes up sees nothing but the debris made by his own hands. Who is his employer he does not know. He works for a company. The men above him, whom he obeys, are overseers, whose lives are as little picturesque as his own. But the squatter lives among leaves and grass, and has daily in his ears the notes of the birds. They are not very musical, these Australian songsters; but neither are they discordant. Their tones are generally plaintive rather than jocund; but they tell of the country, and add a charm to life which is felt rather than appreciated by the squatter and his surroundings.

I purpose in this letter to describe the squatter's position and his life, as they are in all these colonies, and in my next to speak of those whom he employs. In the first place it must be understood that the normal squatter is a lessee of land, and not necessarily an owner. As he comes to possess large tracts of his own, so does he cease to be a squatter in the proper sense of the word, although his pursuits may not be in any way changed. When the thing first began, the importers and breeders of sheep were allowed to run their flocks wherever they found grasses. By degrees it became necessary to divide and limit the pastures of this and that patriarch, so that each might know where his own rights ceased; and then, as funds were required for the general uses of the colonies, it was perceived that as he used the public territory for his own private purposes he should pay something for the use. Hence a system of rentals was instituted, and the squatters became tenants under the Crown. As a different system of land laws prevails in each colony, and as, in each, that system is very intricate, I shall not attempt to explain them within the limits of this letter. As I am writing from New South Wales, I will say that here, on an average, twopence a year is paid for the pasturage of each sheep. A squatter beginning his work may either buy a run—as the tract which he occupies is called—or may take one up by driving his sheep back to land not as yet used. Should he do the latter, some rough survey is made as to the capabilities of the land, and he is charged accordingly. This, however, is hard work. He has to take himself to a country far away from civilisation, to which stores can with difficulty be conveyed, and from which the carriage of his wool must necessarily be tedious and expensive. But he gets the right of occupying his land without the payment of any sum down; and is, for many years, secured by his position from the inroads of his natural enemy, the free selector. Why the free selector should be his enemy, I hope I may be able to explain before I have finished this letter. If he buys a run—and runs are in the market much more commonly than estates with us at home—he is safe from the squatters. As long as he pays his moderate rent he is safe in his holding—should no one else desire to buy a portion of it. The normal price of land belonging to the Crown in New South Wales, and indeed in these colonies generally, is £1 an acre; and as but little of his land is worth so much, it will not be bought from under him in block. But any one may select, on his run or on any other, an amount of land not exceeding 320 acres. As this selection gives the purchaser the right of pasturage over 960 other acres, the squatter in fact loses the use of two square miles of country. As he may probably occupy over a hundred square miles, the loss to him would not be very much were it not that the selector naturally chooses the best of the land. And this invader is not required to pay £1 per acre in ready money. To encourage the growth of a race of yeomen farmers, the law permits him to enter upon his land on paying 5s. an acre. Then in three years he is free, and after that is called upon only for 5 per cent. each year on the remainder. He must, however, live on his land; and unless by the end of the first three years he has improved it to a certain specified extent, he loses it.

Of all free selectors the squatter himself is the greatest. He has the same privileges as others, and always exercises his privilege. It is necessary, in the first place, that he should buy the land on which his homestead and wool-shed stand; and as he will wish to keep other selectors as far from him as possible, he will endeavour to extend his area of purchased property. We have all heard that a skilful practitioner will generally find himself able to drive a coach and horses through an act of Parliament, and the squatters have been very skilful in treating the land laws of their colonial Parliaments after this fashion. He buys the extent of land allowed to himself, and other portions for his father, and children, and brothers, and sisters. When they have been all supplied, he creates other brothers and other sisters, and thus, under a system which is called dummying, he gathers together a considerable estate, which is thus secured from the invasion of other free selectors. The object of the various legislatures has been to prevent the formation of large landed estates, with the view of preventing that inequality of possessions which prevails in the old countries, but legislation has altogether failed in the attempt. There is probably no country in the world in which, in another century, territorial magnificence will prevail to a greater extent than in Australia generally. The land has been cheap, and the rich men have bought it in spite of the laws, and the wealth which has enabled them to buy it has been produced almost entirely by pastoral pursuits.

The squatter proper is, however, still the tenant of the Crown, by which it is intended to be understood that the rent which he pays is a part of the public revenue of the colony. If he be a rich man he is probably also an old man, and owns many runs, and lives himself in Melbourne or Sydney, employing deputy patriarchs to manage his flocks and herds. His life is comfortable, often luxurious and uninteresting enough. The lesser squatter, who perhaps at 35 years of age may own 20,000 sheep, lives on his own, having all the authority, responsibility, and freedom of a modern Abraham. His station is perhaps 40 miles distant from the next town, and half that from his nearest squatter neighbour. The number I have named is small, and yet, if he live in the centre of his run, he must ride five miles before he can get off his own sheep-walk. A run with 200,000 sheep is not rare, and your readers will be able to multiply the distances for themselves.

If he is fond of his business, he does not want to travel frequently beyond his own limits. To do so is a trouble to him, as he is not at home in a city. Nor is there much of the business proper to himself which can be done there. His ewes will take three months to lamb, and he must be at home with them. This will begin in June, the first month of the Australian winter, and the ceremony will not be over much before the end of August. Then come the preparations for washing and shearing, and by the end of September he will have commenced those two great operations of the year. He will hardly get his wool packed and sent away from the station down to the sea-coast much before the middle of December. Then he is in the middle of summer, and the middle of summer in New South Wales is very hot. As to the manner in which fires come, squatters differ in opinion. Some think that they create themselves, which I do not believe, as I can hear of no traces of such fires before the advent of white men. Others attribute them to accidental circumstances, which, though they are accidents, are sure to occur again and again. No shepherd, no stockman, no driver of a team of bullocks, stirs about the bush without a box of matches in his pocket, and very few travel far without a pipe in their mouths. In the middle of summer the slightest spark will set the dry grasses blazing. But then, again, the state of things renders revenge so perilously easy to the dismissed servant or the rejected wanderer, or the sheep-stealer who has been prosecuted. A lighted match is dropped, and the thing is done. The man is travelling alone through the bush—it should be understood that the whole country is called the bush—and is altogether beyond the reach of detection. But the squatter, who in these latter days will probably have fenced his run—that is, have divided his sheep-walk into vast paddocks of six or seven thousand acres each, by sixty or seventy miles of bush fencing—looks upon a fire on his run as almost the greatest evil which can befall him. The squatter who does his own work on a small run cannot be absent during the intense heat of the summer. Then there will be fears of drought, against which he provides by tanks and dams which require watching; fears of deficient grass, which is apt, when he most wants grass, to be invaded by kangaroos and wild horses. There was not a horse in Australia a hundred years ago, but now there are herds containing hundreds running wild in the bush. Sheep, too, are subject to many maladies, as to all of which the head squatter has to be doctor in chief. It will sometimes happen that every foot of 10,000 sheep will have to be treated separately. The big man will do all this by deputy. The more that can be done adequately by deputy, the better for the owner. But the young struggling master of flocks, who cannot afford the presence of a second self, feels that his own presence on the run is at all times indispensable. When away he is nervous and unhappy. And there has grown upon him at home a feeling of mastership over everything around him, which he is hardly comfortable in losing among a crowd.

At home, as I have said, he has many troubles; but the worst of all his troubles is the free selector. In many respects this is unreasonable, but it is very natural. I cannot now go into the original quarrel between the squatters and the legislators, or tell the reasons why, in the different colonies, the owners of sheep felt that faith was not kept with them. The story would be too long for your columns. But the squatter of to-day knows, and the squatter for the last fifteen years has known, that he held his own subject to selection. He will always say that to the genuine selector, the man who will live by farming or eke out his living by labour, he has no antipathy. He would rather be without him: if, however, such a one come, he shall not be treated as an enemy. But the free selector who does come—so says the squatter—cannot live by farming and does not mean to work for wages. He has one of two objects, or probably both. So says the squatter. He will steal sheep, or make himself in other ways so disagreeable that the squatter will be forced to buy him out. There are men among this class who do steal sheep, and the prospect of being bought out at a profit is, no doubt, present to the free-selecting mind. And when a man does steal sheep, convictions are very difficult. The juries are not unfrequently in the selector's favour, and there is a feeling here, as elsewhere, antagonistic to the aristocrat. The squatter is supposed to be big enough to take care of himself. Of the free selector generally I will speak further in my next letter; but from what I have said it may be understood that the enmity should be strong. Nevertheless, as a rule, the squatter is big enough to take care of himself. There is, too, no duty more manifestly incumbent on the big man than that of bearing, if not with patience, at any rate with dignity, the evils which come from the inferiority of the lesser man.

The squatter's home is not luxurious, but it is generally very plentiful. He not only kills his own meat and makes his own bread, but supplies meat and flour to every one on his station. Meat and flour, tea and sugar, make up the regular rations of the hands on the station, but the squatter is supposed to keep a store from which he can provide not only all that his own family may require, but everything that a shearer or a shepherd may be disposed to purchase. If a man wants a pair of moleskin trousers or a box of lucifer matches, he presumes that the squatter should supply him, and charge him with the price when the wages are settled.

One thing, however, he can never buy. No squatter would supply his men with strong drink.

The home of the squatter is unique of its kind. Sometimes it is very large—but it is large not by the size of the building, but by the multiplication of buildings. It seldom rises above the ground story, and is always furnished with a verandah, in which his wife passes perhaps the greater part of her time. The kitchen is a separate house; and then as the need for further accommodation increases, other little houses are built. There is always a cottage for the young men about the station and for travelling guests, and a hut for working men and travellers of that class. Thus with stables, coachhouse, bathroom, and the like, there grows up a little village which is called The Station.

As the life of the squatter is much mixed up with that of those who work under him, I shall have to say something further of the manner of his life in my next letter.

Letter XIV

IN MY LAST LETTER I attempted to describe the life of the working squatter in the Australian colonies. In this I purpose to speak of the rural labourer—whose condition is by far the more important of the two, as hundreds come out yearly with the intention of making their way by the work of their hands, whereas those who emigrate with money in their pockets, intending to make their fortunes by growing wool, are comparatively few.

Men who emigrate without capital, hoping to earn by their work better bread in the colonies than they can do at home, generally fall into one of four classes. I have spoken of miners and their earnings, and of those who are employed in trades and as servants in the town. The greater number of such men, however, find their way into the rural districts, on to the vast grazing grounds of the colonies, and become either the servants of the squatters, or else free selectors of land on the squatters' runs. The man who goes out altogether penniless, and with no skill in any trade, will become first a labourer, and then, if things go well with him, and his ambition lie in that direction, he will take up land as his own. No doubt this is the most usual condition of the intending emigrant; and as the work of a shepherd is easier to learn than any other, he will probably become a shepherd before he has been long in the colony.

A man soon after his arrival may probably find himself engaged to travel with what he will here call a "mob of sheep," perhaps three or four thousand, and to assist in taking them over a distance of 500 miles. In doing so he will learn much of the nature of sheep, and much also of the nature of the colonies, and after two or three such journeys will feel himself entitled to drop the name of a "new chum," which will be given to him during his noviciate. At this work he will be paid at a rate varying from £30 to £50 per annum, according to his experience and capacity. But that money will be all profit to him, excepting the very moderate expenditure necessary for his clothes. His food will be found for him, and he will soon become habituated to having his food, or rations, always at his hand without purchase on his part. He will often have to cook them and to make his own bread; but tea and sugar, flour and meat, will be supplied to him as certainly as is the light of the sun, and he will soon learn to regard them equally as the natural accessories of life. The weekly allowance made to him will be ¼ lb. of tea, 2 lb. of sugar, 10 lb. of flour, and 14 lb. of meat. The meat he will frequently be obliged to salt. The flour he must make into damper over a wood fire. But there will be the provisions, and he will find them ample. At the work of which I am now speaking he will probably have four or five companions, one of whom will be told off as cook. If he have any rough gifts that way himself—in which gifts must be included the arts of killing and skinning sheep and oxen—he will find them by no means thrown away in a grazing life. His sheep will travel about five miles a day; and as they will not pass along confined roads, it will be his peculiar duty to know them by their marks and to see that they do not get mixed—or, in colonial language, boxed—with the sheep belonging to the lands through which he passes. I cannot say that the life is a life of enterprise, but it has more of difficulty, and, therefore, more of excitement, than would at first be thought. For about three months these men will be without a roof, travelling through endless forests or over vast plains, bivouacking at night over a wood fire, killing the weaker of their flock for food as it is wanted, followed by a cart with their flour and sugar, smoking a great deal of tobacco, drinking a great deal of tea, but tasting probably not a drop of strong drink from the beginning to the end of the long journey. When the work is accomplished, the wages for the whole time are paid by a cheque; and if the recipient of the cheque can then also restrain himself from strong drink, he may soon, if he so pleases, drive sheep of his own.

There are various classes of work on a squatter's run. A man may, and very often does, become simply a shepherd. The work is very easy, but terribly monotonous, and so lonely as to lead not unfrequently to insanity. There are two ways of pasturing sheep. They are either followed by shepherds over unenclosed plains—which is the old-fashioned way, and is still continued in many districts—or they are confined within enclosures called paddocks. The shepherd is required for the former mode of grazing. He has his hut, where he lives alone, and follows his flock from morning till about four o'clock, when the sheep of their own accord will draw up to their sleeping-ground, close to his abode. Once a week, or perhaps only once a fortnight, his food will be brought to him—such rations as I have already named—and beyond this he will see no one. Tobacco will be his solace, and religion, or rather religious fears, will too often be his bugbear. He will be paid about £40 per annum—more or less, according to his capacity, and the number of sheep entrusted to him; and his consolation should consist in this, that he may put by all his wages, and at the end of three years start with money in his pocket as a buyer of land. But, alas, the strength for such perseverance as that is so seldom within the reach of a shepherd.

But the squatter who divides his run into paddocks—vast enclosures of from 6000 to 12,000 acres—also requires men. He cannot leave either his sheep or his fences unwatched, and employs men whose business it is always to be on horseback. They see the sheep out on to the pastures in the morning, and again at their camp at night, and should be especially careful that no breach in the fences is left unrepaired. These men also live generally alone in huts, but, from the fact of their being mounted, they see their fellow-creatures much more frequently. Such a man will receive about £5 per annum more than a shepherd, and will have his horses found for him. But he, too, must do everything for himself; must cook his own meat, and salt it, and make his own bread, and live alone out in the forest, with no human being probably within half-a-dozen miles of him. This man is generally called a boundary-rider, and his condition is better than that of the simple shepherd.

There is very much work that is always done by contract at these stations, and which requires, indeed, a certain amount of skill, but not skill of a very high order. Timber is felled and cleared at so much an acre, the amount paid of course varying with the nature of the wood. Water dams are made. Miles upon miles of rough fencing are put up, at so much a mile. And here and there patches of land are redeemed from grazing purposes and turned to cultivation. What a man can earn at this work will of course depend on his skill and industry, but with an average man it will seldom be less than 5s. a day. When so employed, he must buy his own food, which, however, he will get at certain fixed prices from the squatter who employs him. Rations such as I have named above will cost him about 8s. a week. He can buy other comforts if he wants them—almost anything, indeed, except strong drink. Currants for plum-dumplings, pickles, and jam, are the luxuries most general on a station.

But there is a harvest season among sheep as well as with hay and corn; and for those who can work at the harvest, wages are higher than at other times, and work is of course heavier. The harvest time consists of the washing and shearing of sheep, and of the pressing of wool. Three months in the year are occupied with these labours, though it will not often happen that so long a period will be taken at any one stretch. September, October, and November may be named as these months, though there will be some variation according to the climates of the different colonies. At washing sheep, men will earn about 20s. a week and their rations. It is hard, sloppy, disagreeable work, but it has, at any rate, the comfort of being done gregariously. Six or a dozen men will be together; and when the work is over, and they have put on their dry trousers, they can eat their plum-puddings and mutton chops, drink their tea, and smoke their tobacco in all the luxury of company.

But the work in the wool-shed is the work of the year, and very hard it is—perhaps as fatiguing work as a man can put his hand to till he becomes perfectly used to it. And it is not every man who can shear— not every man who can even with practice. There is a certain skill in the manipulation of the hand which it seems that some men cannot acquire. A man, at any rate to become an expert shearer, should begin early in life, and should have learned the trade by the time that he is four or five-and-twenty. Shearing is, of course, done by task-work; and the men are paid by the 100 sheep. The amount paid will vary according to the colony, or the district of the colony, in which the work is to be done; but the average rate is about 17s. 6d. a-hundred. Of course, it is very much to the interest of the men to shear as many sheep in the day as possible; and it is equally to the interest of the squatter to have them shorn quickly—provided they are well shorn. But here there is apt to arise a difference of opinion, which has sometimes to be settled in a rough fashion. It will be the ambition of the practical shearer to turn a hundred shorn sheep into his pen each day; and shearers have done more than this; but in quick shearing the sheep will sometimes be frightfully mutilated, and patches of wool will sometimes be left on their back. Then the squatter, or the foreman of the wool-shed, is driven to interfere, and to tell his too rapid workman that he must shear more slowly or leave the shed. I have known cases in which a man has declined to do either unless he was paid for what sheep he had shorn up to that time. But the squatter's contract is that he will pay for nothing till the work is done, lest his men should leave him, seeking some other wool-shed before his shearing is over. In such a case, the squatter has to be his own policeman, and there may be a difficulty. But the men as a rule are fair, and will generally stand by their employer if there be a fair allowance of give and take on each side. An average shearer should pass 60 sheep a day through his hands, and in this way he will earn 10s. 6d. a-day, or £3 3s. a-week.

A wool-shed at shearing time, with perhaps sixty or seventy men at work upon it, is a pretty sight; though I can imagine there may be those who would find their sense of smell offended. The sheep are enclosed in pens in the middle, from whence they are drawn by the shearers on to the board. Each shearer may have a space about four feet broad, on which he turns his victim on his back, and dispossesses him of his coat in about seven or eight minutes. Then the bare animal is allowed to escape into a pen which is the peculiar property of the shearer, so that he may know and certify his own numbers. If he cuts a sheep, he is bound to apply some salve of medicinal tar, and to become the surgeon to the wound he has inflicted. Boys are employed to remove the fleeces as quickly as they are shorn, and to take them to the sorting table. The shearer therefore does not move from his board till the happy hour arrives for a smoke or for dinner, or the still happier hour of release for the evening.

The shearer generally feeds himself—that is to say, he is charged by the squatter for the rations he consumes. A cook is employed, or at large wool-sheds two or three cooks, for whom the shearers pay 2s. 6d. a head per week; and to this functionary they are merciless. Hot bread, hot buns, hot puddings, and hot meat are required three times a day, not to speak of tea, which is supposed to be ready at all times. In the evening they are jolly enough, if, as is usual, they have some men among their number capable of singing songs or telling stories. The difference among men in this respect is very remarkable, there being some who seem never willing to open their mouths except for purposes of sternest necessity, while others are gifted with a run of wit and animal vivacity which never deserts them. It will be said that there is the same difference in all classes. No doubt. But with these men the dull man is subjected to no discredit, nor does the witty man achieve any great reputation.

So much for the wages and life of men upon stations. Instead of getting among sheep a man may get among cattle, and his life and prospects will be very much the same. The interesting point is this, that if a man be sober and fairly industrious he may at the end of the year have put by £30, and have had plenty to eat during the time. Men who read this, or who hear these tidings at home, will be sure of their own industry and of their own sobriety. I will now return to tell my readers what I have found to be the case so often as to constitute—I will not say the rule, for that word would be too strong, but a state of things so common as to make one almost fear to recommend men to come out to this land of plenty.

I have said that the workman, not only during his hour of work, but also during his days, and weeks, and months of work, is debarred from drink. This is so much the fashion of the country that the men do not think of it or seem to want it. At shearing time it is part of the contract that there shall be no intoxicating liquor on the place; and throughout the ordinary work of the year it never comes in their way. There is no feeling, as there is with us, that a man cannot get through his labour without his beer. So far the whole question as to strong drink seems to be settled in a manner that would satisfy Sir Wilfrid Lawson.[30] But then comes the period of danger. The man receives the cheque for his past work—perhaps wages for half a year—and feels that some indulgence, some pleasure, is due to him for his industry and forbearance. He consequently takes his cheque to a publican, to whom he entrusts it, and proceeds at once, in his own phrase,

[30] Sir Wilfrid Lawson (1829–1906), a famed prohibitionist and radical reformer.

to "knock it down." If the game is pleasant to him, it is doubly so to the publican. The man, of course, is soon drunk, and is kept in that state perhaps for a week or more, till the publican's conscience, vacillating between the probability of killing him and of robbing him too outrageously, thinks fit to say that the cheque has been duly knocked down, and that the man must go and tramp forth in search of further work. The wretch is turned out, perhaps, in the horrors of delirium tremens, and goes through a period of agony which would, one would think, warn him for the future. But after a while he is again at his work, again receives his cheque, and again knocks it down—till he comes to look upon that as the regular routine of life. At the public house the men drink nothing but spirits, and spirits adulterated in the most nefarious fashion. Many, of course, are killed by it, while many more sink from year to year to a condition in which they will own that they know their case to be hopeless.

In my next letter I will endeavour to tell your readers what may be, and what is, done by the system of free selection of land.

Letter XV

IT HAS BEEN strongly felt by the governing men in all
the Australian colonies, that the possession of freehold land would be the greatest allurement to emi-
grators from home, and would at the same time create
a class of colonists more useful and trustworthy than
any other. A man who has acquired property has
given a great pledge for good conduct, and a man who
owns landed property is seldom ready for immediate
flight. To get a population, and to keep it, has been the
object of the governing bodies, and it has come to be
acknowledged in the management of colonial affairs
that the best mode of doing this is to induce men to
settle on patches of land which they can regard as
their own.

Your space would not allow me to go back to the
early features of this question; nor does my purpose,
in regard to the present system of free selection in
these colonies, require it. Grants of land, very large in
amount, were at first made, under certain circumstances, of which your readers can learn the details
elsewhere, if they require to know them. And land in
larger quantities was, as it is called, "taken up" by
squatters, thereby becoming in no degree their property; but in this way the squatters obtained a right to
the leasehold occupation of such lands till purchasers
should come forward. But neither of these modes of

occupation had any tendency to create such a body of landowners, or what I may perhaps call such a yeomanry, as was desired. Indeed, they both had a directly contrary tendency, as they threw vast territories into single hands, thereby preventing the spread of a body of small possessors.

Then there arose naturally in all these colonies a very diverse interest. The squatters, of course, became averse to small purchasers, learned to think that the welfare of the colonies would depend on the existence of a rich landed aristocracy—they themselves being, of course, the aristocrats—and complained bitterly of the encroachments which the altered land laws from time to time made in their position. But the men who wished to become owners of small farms—a much more numerous class, but individually less influential, as being less wealthy—taught themselves to regard the squatters as cormorants, who desired to swallow up and monopolise lands which, if properly divided, would suffice to make a nation of happy and independent freeholders. In fact there arose, as was natural, the two old parties, which we used to call Tories and Whigs, and which we now call Conservatives and Liberals. As has always happened in English-speaking communities, the Liberals have carried the day as far as legislation has been concerned, but the Conservatives have kept a secure hold of their wealth and personal influence.

In every Australian colony the right of any comer to purchase crown lands has been recognised and legalised; but in no two colonies has this been done by precisely similar laws. But the idea has always been the same; and though the efforts to effect the object have been made in various ways, the object has been very nearly identical in all. It has been desired that the land should become the freehold possession of the occupier, so that he might feel the strongest possible inducement to remain upon it. And it has been desired also that the amount of land purchasable should be small, so as to be within the power of beneficial occupation by a comparatively poor man; that it should be sold at such a price as to be brought within his means, and that it should be paid for under circumstances that should at the same time be easy and secure. It has also been an essential necessity that the purchaser should live upon his land and occupy it beneficially. And many safeguards have been necessary in this legislation as to the sale of public lands—so many as to make the matter exceedingly complicated. One and the same person must not be allowed to buy two or more lots; one person must not be allowed to buy for the use of another—or to buy for his own use in the name of another. There has been in the arrangement of all these land laws a sincere anxiety to carry out the purpose desired by the colonies at large, but the difficulties have been great. It has been necessary to put vast power into the hands of certain ministers, which power has not always been used for the best purpose; and it has been for the interest of some to perform that well-known feat of driving a coach and horses through these acts of Parliament; and the coaches and horses have been driven through triumphantly. In all these struggles the rich squatters have come off the best, as here, as elsewhere, nothing is so powerful as wealth.

Here in New South Wales, from which colony I am at present writing, a free selector, under the law at this moment existing, may purchase any number of acres not less than 40 and not more than 320, and these he may select on any crown land in the colony not reserved for special purchases. The intending purchaser may wander about the squatter's runs, and when he finds a spot which he fancies will suit his purpose he "pegs out" for himself the quantity he desires, and when he has complied with the demands of the law the squatter has to secede and he enters in upon the land. The price he has to pay is 20s. an acre, of which sum he is called upon for 5s. an acre down. Till this ceremony has been complied with he can do nothing; but when it has been complied with he can do anything. The selector of 100 acres must therefore have £25 in his pocket. Then for three years he makes no payment at all; after that he pays—now at this minute—5 per cent. per annum on the remaining 15s. till he shall please to pay that sum off and become the freehold possessor; but in the meantime no man can dispossess him, and his property in the land is transferable, so that he has all the material advantages of a freehold. By a new law, which is now before the colonial legislature, it is proposed to call upon the free selector to pay off the 15s. at the rate of 1s. an acre per annum. In either one case or the other the demand upon him is very light; and in addition to the land which is so purchased, the purchaser has the right of running his sheep or cattle over three times the number of acres selected; so that the buyer of 100 acres would, for pastoral purposes, have possession of 300 other acres, from which the flocks of the squatter who formerly occupied it are debarred.

A month is allowed to the selector to look about him and to build a hut. After that he must reside upon his land, and during his first three years he must expend 20s. an acre on improvements. Of course there are here great facilities and great temptations to evade the law. It is difficult to say what is residence, and almost impossible to go beyond the declaration of the selector as to the money spent; but such are the enactments made with the view of ensuring the desired object.

As it is my intention here to tell a man how he may avail himself of the law, and not how he may evade it, I will presume that the selector at any rate intends to comply with it. I have shown that a man may enter in upon his 100 acres for £25; but unless he has other money in his pocket his land will be of very little use to him. I have explained also—in the last letter which I wrote to you—that an industrious and sober man in this country, a man who is not afraid of work, and is fairly clever with his hands, can look forward to have £70 or £80 in his pocket at the end of three years. I must say again here that, in order to effect this, the man must be not only industrious but sober also. That he should do his work without drink will be a necessity of his position. What will be required of him is that, when his work is over, he shall be able to deny himself the indulgence in filthy orgies which will be resorted to by many of his companions.

When the selector has his land, he will no doubt feel considerable difficulty as to what he should do with it. The great deficiency here seems to be the want of some director by which the man may know where to select—such as I explained in one of my former letters to be now provided for him in Western Australia. The man, during his years of experience as a paid labourer, will have learned much, and before he chooses his spot will have his own ideas. One man will think that he can live by running a few hundred sheep, or a few score of bullocks—which, if the man is and desires to remain honest, is, perhaps, of all modes of living on his land which he can select, the most dangerous. The temptation to steal the sheep of the great squatters around him will be very great, and the sin of stealing them will be terribly reduced in his eyes by the frequency of the offence around him. Another will perhaps attempt to grow wheat for the markets—and may thrive after that fashion, if he will first have learned not only what land will carry wheat, but also what land may be expected to ripen the crop often enough to pay him for his work. In South Australia, a very large number of men live by growing wheat on selected lands; and, though their life is rough, it is plentiful. They who do best in this colony are, I think, men who have found their land near enough to the provincial towns to supply them with milk, butter, potatoes, oats, and such produce as a community is sure to demand. But perhaps the most natural life into which a free selector may fall, and on the whole the most beneficial, is that of being part freeholder and part labourer. He should remember when he begins that he cannot hope to make money by paying for other labour than his own. If he have sons who can work for him and live with him, sharing his toils and his abundance, it may be very well; but till he arrive at that state of blessedness he must do everything with his own hands, or with those of a partner. He must pay no money wages, unless he shall himself have earned money wages to enable him to do so. Even in that event, the prudent man will be anxious to keep what he has received. If he will work for others during three months of the year—condescending to take the squatter's money and to be the squatter's man for that period—then he can afford to eat the potatoes he will grow, and to consume his own milk and butter; and the squatter's money will pay for those things for which money is absolutely needed, till his land shall have been cleared and cropped throughout, and he shall be able to live entirely on his own property.

For he must remember—this intending free selector—that the land, when he has got possession of it on paying his 5s. an acre, will not be at once fit for the plough, so that he may hope to reap in the first summer as many acres as he can afford to sow. It will probably be covered with timber, and will at any rate demand much rough work before it will produce him crops that he can sell. He must have capital for his first year's living, and then let him eke that out by earning wages during a portion of the year.

I have spoken of the natural aversion felt by the squatter to the system of free selection; but as the eels become used to skinning, so have the squatters become used to their unwelcome neighbours. The squatter of the present day will prefer that no free selector should come within his limits; but he is generally, I think, prepared to be a good neighbour to the man who comes, if the man will be a good neighbour to him. Free selection is a necessity, and he is prepared to make the best of it; and the rascally free selector is so intolerable a nuisance to him, that he is well disposed to the man who has settled himself down with the idea of making an honest living, and of taking no more than the law allows him.

No man can visit this country and look into the question without seeing that there is much ground for the complaints made against very many of the free selectors. Character has nothing to do with selection; a thief at large may buy land as he may tea and sugar in the shops, and many thieves do buy land solely in order that they may live on their neighbours by dishonest practices. They have no idea of honest work, but are aware that they can make themselves so intensely disagreeable to a man of property as to compel their rich neighbours to buy them off. They steal sheep, and it is almost impossible to trace such sheep when stolen. They steal cattle and they steal horses, and they keep unlicensed houses in which they sell abominable liquor to the hands about the station. In this way a class of idle, utterly unprincipled men is created, which is a curse to the colony, and sometimes so severe a thorn in the sides of a squatter as to drive him from his holding. Their crimes, too, become so common that they almost cease to be odious in the eyes of a great portion of the community. Nothing can be so deleterious to a people at large as a lax feeling in regard to general honesty. Rogues in the world do not do half so much injury by their roguery as by creating indifference to honesty in the minds of men who are not rogues. It is not thieving, direct thieving, which hurts us so much as an absence of that general indignation which thieving should engender. The stealing of sheep has here become so common that men who never steal sheep themselves—to whom the stealing of a sheep would be a thing not to be thought of—become indifferent to it in others, and think it venial. The squatter has so many that surely he can bear to lose a few! It is almost considered to be the free selector's privilege, or at any rate his perquisite, to live on his rich neighbour's mutton. As one consequence of this feeling, juries in the small towns are most unwilling to convict, the sympathies of jurymen being generally with the selectors. Hence it has arisen that the squatter feels so acute an injury when he hears that a new-coming free selector has settled on his run.

But in spite of all this, I regard free selection—or rather the purchase of land in small quantities by men who will live upon it and cultivate it themselves—as the system on which these colonies must chiefly depend for their permanent prosperity. And to the young labourer at home, the man of some intelligence and much self-reliance, I look upon the chance so offered to him as the best which there is within his reach. He may avoid the evils which I have endeavoured to point out, and if he does so there is open to him here the life of an independent yeoman.

But let me say once more that that life will not be within his reach unless he can eschew the raptures of a public house.

Letter XVI

IN MY LATE LETTERS I have spoken of the colonies of Victoria and New South Wales which I have now visited. I also said a few words of Western Australia as I was passing by it. The other Australian colonies, as your readers no doubt are aware, are Tasmania, South Australia, and Queensland. Though I have not now returned to them, it may be as well that I should say something of their condition and prospects.

Though it is now nearly twenty years since the name was changed, there are still many in England who will more readily recognise Tasmania under the name of Van Diemen's Land. Botany Bay and Van Diemen's Land were the two words which used to bring to our mind our Australian convict settlements, and it was simply as a convict settlement that the island lying at the south-eastern point of Australia was first used. When it was found that the number of convicts sent out could not be safely employed and taken care of in the districts round Sydney, a subsidiary establishment was founded here in 1804, which as a convict establishment was eminently serviceable to the mother country, and which served that purpose up to 1853. Then the free settlers in the island became stronger in their influence than the curators of the distant British gaol, and the island succeeded in repudiating the ig-nominious uses to which it had been put, as New South

Wales had done before. Then too it was felt that the name of Van Diemen's Land had been stained with ruffianism, and the pretty appellation of Tasmania was given to it.

But the convict establishment in a modified form still exists. When that at Sydney was abolished, the convicts then there were taken to Van Diemen's Land; but there was no place to which those from the latter place could be sent when it turned over a new leaf and was re-christened. It was therefore necessary that the men should be maintained there till they were emancipated or had died out. As a consequence there are still in the island some few of the worst scoundrels that ever England produced. Till a year or two ago they were kept in isolation at Port Arthur—a most wonderful place, almost an island, and probably the most picturesque spot ever selected as an enforced home for felons. But now the numbers, which in the course of nature have decreased, are too small for the expenditure necessary for such an establishment, and the men have been removed to ordinary gaols. In this way the stain of Van Diemen's Land has now nearly worn itself out.

In 1856 Tasmania followed her greater colonial sisters in claiming and obtaining the right of self-government. Since that time, though it is but a little place—with about 100,000 inhabitants, which number, if it increases at all, increases very slowly[31]—it has had its King, Lords, and House of Commons under the names of Governor, Legislative Council, and Assembly. Brit-

[31] Tasmania continues to grow only very slowly. Its present population is about 230,000.

ish colonies with very much smaller numbers have commenced their work under the same system, and have thriven heartily. Queensland had not above a quarter of the number when she began; and New Zealand was very far from boasting so great a population. But in these colonies young life was throbbing with vast impulses. They possessed that energy which a consciousness of present success always gives. But Tasmania has never been alive as have New Zealand and Queensland.

But still Tasmania struggles on, and holds its own. There is, no doubt, on the part of Victoria, to which it is adjacent, a desire to annex the island, and so to swell her own borders, her own population, and her own importance. And there are bribes which it can and does hold out to Tasmania. At present a cruel system of protective duties shuts out the produce of Tasmania from the large markets of Victoria. And this debars the farmers and fruit-growers of the island from the consumers to whom they should naturally look. These duties would of course cease if the two colonies became one. And then that establishment of king, lords, and commons, with judges and other paraphernalia, of its own, costs money, which would be spared if Tasmania were merely a province of Victoria. But still Tasmania loves her own independence, and would be loth to become merely an appanage of a younger sister, of whom she is very jealous.

The merits of the question would require more space than can be found in the fraction of a letter such as this; but it may be as well to suggest here that a time must probably come when there will be a customs union between all these colonies, and after that a general federal union for the purposes of a joint government. To an Englishman, who looks on Australia as a whole, and as one of the most happy attempts which have ever been made in the art of colonisation, it seems absurd that Victoria and South Australia, or New South Wales and Queensland, should look upon themselves as separate nationalities and with separate interests, and almost hostile ambitions; and to be a mad thing that they should charge customs duties each on the produce of the other. That some such union will come there can, I think, be but little doubt. But the greater the number of such colonies or states, the quicker will they probably unite. It is not by adding to the superiority of one which is already the richest and the greatest that the union will be the most readily achieved.

Tasmania is much more like England than are the other colonies. Its climate is more like our own, as it is further from the tropics, and therefore also its products. It is especially a land of fruits. It produces hops and oats in great abundance, and wheat also, though not with the same assurance of success. The scenery here is very lovely, which cannot be said generally of the larger land. A great part of it is still perfectly wild, containing no inhabitants, no cattle, no sheep, and hitherto producing nothing. Enormous primeval forests still stretch through the south-western counties, which probably have never yet been visited by Europeans.

Wages are a little, but only a very little, lower than in Victoria or New South Wales; but work is not so readily found. Provisions are something lower, and the labourer who has employment may live as well here as in the larger colonies.

The history of South Australia is altogether unlike that of the other Australian colonies. They were all in some measure established by operation of the government at home. Victoria and Queensland no doubt separated themselves from New South Wales by their own energies; but before such separation they had been colonised under the influence and by the handling of the Colonial Office at home. South Australia may almost be said to have become a colony in opposition to the Colonial Office, and she can boast that no British convict, as a convict, has ever been placed on her soil.

Captain Sturt, than whom no one holds a more honourable place in the band of Australian explorers, in 1829 made his way down the Murrumbidgee and Murray rivers, in a little boat which he had carried across the country for that purpose, till he found that the great central Australian waters—the two great rivers which I have named with the Darling, which runs into the Murray—make their way into the sea through a mouth which is altogether unfit for the purposes of navigation. It was a great disappointment— not the less so as at that moment there was every chance that he would lose his life in the enterprise. But he did make his way back again, and the report which he made as to lands which he had seen to the westward of the southern bend of the Murray instigated the first attempt on the part of certain philanthropists to establish that colony which we now call South Australia. A company was formed at home for creating a new settlement with new laws, with a new benevolent prospectus, under which men were to be enabled to colonise with all the advantages which the experience of the older colonies could give them, but with absolute freedom from any of the old defects. The history of the failures—for they were very great failures—and of the amount of success which was ultimately achieved cannot be written here. But it is a history very interesting to those who still think that, if the right way could only be found, some happy Utopia might yet be established on earth in which there should be no want, no injustice, and no suffering. Such a Utopia certainly was not found in the new colony called South Australia. There were periods in its early days in which those who had led the way were almost driven to doubt whether its failure would not be specially disastrous; but after a while it turned the corner, and has thriven since with fair average success. No visitor there now would see in its condition any special results of the philosophy and philanthropy of its founders; but he would find a diligent population living in plenty, and some few, who have reached the top, making large fortunes. The same may be said of all these colonies, if we except poor Western Australia and poor Tasmania.

The growth of wool is the staple trade of South Australia, as it is of Australia generally. The central plains which stretch away to the north till they reach the limits which are yet known are salt in their nature, and on that account peculiarly fit for sheep; but they are subject to great droughts. The results of the trade are therefore precarious, but are often great. But there have been two other great sources of wealth in the colony. It is especially a wheat-growing country, and therefore adapted to the farmer who has a small capital and is capable of working either by his own hands or by those of his sons. There is a special class of such men here—who are perhaps not honoured in that they are called "cockatoos," because they are supposed to scratch the ground on which they live rather than to till it—who own their own land, and for the most part cultivate it with their own hands. The farmer ploughs his land, sows it, and then gathers his harvest by a machine called a stripper, which not only reaps the corn from the land, but also strips the corn from the ear. The straw is left on the land and burned. The same thing is done on the same land year after year, till it will produce no more, and then other land is sought. It is not farming of a high class, but it enables the colony to produce twice the wheat which it consumes, and to be the granary of the colonies around which cannot feed themselves. Within the last ten years the produce has ranged as high as 14 bushels 20 pounds per acre, and as low as 4 bushels 40 pounds, and the price to the producer will vary from a little over to a little under 5s. a bushel. To an English farmer these results will not appear great; but he must remember that the ground has been purchased on credit, at a price varying from 20s. to 40s. an acre, and that the owner has worked it at a minimum of cost. The cockatoo farmer of South Australia lives a plentiful but not a picturesque life, and unless he gets hopelessly into debt is his own master.

South Australia has also been fortunate in having an almost unlimited supply of copper within her limits. As Victoria, New South Wales, and Queensland are golden, so is South Australia especially a copper colony. The Burra-Burra mines, and after them the mines at Wallaroo and Moonta, have been the source of enormous wealth to individuals, and of course at the same time of much general prosperity.

In speaking of South Australia it would be hardly fair not to mention Adelaide, its capital, which is one of the pleasantest towns among the colonies, well built, well adorned, and surrounded by gardens. I have seen no new town that has a greater look of general average prosperity.[32] Nor should I forget to mention that to this colony, which at present has a population of less than 200,000 inhabitants, Australia generally is indebted for the enterprise which carried telegraph wires through the vast deserts of the continent to the northern shores, and so connected all the colonies with the mother country. Its name is certainly a misnomer, for its limits run from south to north through the entire land, but do not comprise the most southern of Australian lands, which lie within the precincts of Victoria.

Queensland, which lies to the north of New South

[32] The city of Adelaide itself today shelters 312,617 persons.

Wales, is a hot country, the northern half of it lying within the tropics. Victoria had been separated from New South Wales in 1850, and Tasmania in 1856. Queensland, therefore—or the district of Moreton Bay, as it was called, for the name of Queensland was not then known—could not endure to be an appanage, and also demanded separation, having only 15,000 inhabitants when she first put forward the demand. In 1859 the concession was made, and the experiment has certainly been justified by success. The Queenslanders are loud-mouthed confident colonists, who have justified their boasting by their action. There are now about 150,000 of them,[33] and they are an enterprising, wealthy people, who are not likely to come to want, although they are saddled with the enormous debt of £32 10s. per head. In South Australia, of which I have just spoken, it amounts to £19 a head, and in Tasmania to something over £14.

Queensland has been one of the colonies which have been the richest in gold—the gold reefs running apparently through the eastern parts of the continent. Gympie was very rich and very great; but now there is a rumour that the gold which is being found on the Palmer River within the York Peninsula will prove to be the richest which Australia has produced. But the York Peninsula lies high within the tropics, and is very hot; and the same rumour says that the work is unfit for Europeans, and that many of those who have gone there in quest of wealth have succumbed to the cli-

[33] Queensland has grown very rapidly, and now has a population of about 1,000,000.

mate. If it be so, the Palmer River gold will be an El Dorado for the Chinese, who have found the way to Queensland, who can stand the heat, and have shown themselves to be indefatigable in the search for gold.

The heat of Queensland and the climate have made the colony in some respects very different from its sisters. It produces sugar early and will produce it very abundantly. But sugar cannot be grown by white labour. It is too costly, and the European cannot stand the heat. Hence there has sprung up the greatly vexed question of imported labour. In Queensland, men have been brought in from some of the South Sea Islands, whose services have been invaluable. It may indeed be said that without some such labour articles of tropical produce cannot be grown in the colony. But such necessity will not justify the employment of these men on any terms which are not beneficial to themselves. It certainly will not gratify the kidnapping of men or any arrangement of labour which has about it a savour of slavery. Men have been kidnapped from the islands and made to work almost as slaves, if not in Queensland, yet in other lands on that side of the world. There is, I think, no doubt that this has been done at Fiji. Consequently a cry has come up against Queensland which I believe to have been altogether undeserved. The laws for the importation, protection, proper payment, and speedy return of these men are most stringent. From all that I could see there, and from all that I have been able to learn, I doubt whether there are any labourers in any country whose welfare is better secured than that of the

Polynesians in Queensland. But the white labourer there thinks most erroneously that the price of his labour will be reduced by the importation; and hence the cry has come. But in truth the white man cannot do the work for which the South Sea Islander is required.

Queensland, also, is a great wool colony, rivalling Victoria in the magnificence of her squatters. But she is not a corn-producing country. Pine-apples and bananas grow there, as oranges do in New South Wales, and grapes in South Australia, and strawberries and cherries in Tasmania.

Letter XVII

Sydney

IN OCTOBER, 1874—just one year ago when this letter will reach England—Great Britain was strengthened or burdened, as the case may be, by the possession of a new colony. On the 10th of that month, the British flag was hoisted, "with the usual formalities," by Sir Hercules Robinson, in Fiji. Sir Hercules was and is the governor of New South Wales, and had been commissioned by the Home Government to complete the arrangement, if such completion might be possible; and this he did successfully.[34]

There is, I think, at home, a general opinion that Great Britain possesses enough of the world—as much as she can well manage—and that new territorial possessions must be regarded rather as increased burdens than increased strength. No doubt the power of the country and the prestige which belongs to its name are based on its colonial and Indian empire. Every Englishman sufficiently awake to be proud of England feels this; but there is at the same time a general conviction that enough has been done—that we have got all that can do us good, and that we should abstain from taking more, if it be possible to abstain. This certainly was the opinion in regard to Fiji, and the

---

[34] Sir Hercules Robinson (1824–1897) was one of England's greatest nineteenth-century colonial governors. He served successively and successfully as governor of Ceylon, New South Wales, and Cape Colony, South Africa, besides negotiating for the Fiji Islands in 1874. He was made Lord Rosmead in 1896.

proposed annexation was for a time refused. Then gradually there came upon our statesmen at home a conviction that the thing must be done—that, in spite of ourselves, we must, for certain reasons, make ourselves the masters of these islands, and that it was only left for us to consider in what way we might best assume control over the unenvied possession.

Nor is this the first time that we have been so coerced. When we began the task of government in New Zealand, in 1840—for, though the British flag had flown in New Zealand many years before that, it was only then that we really assumed possession of the islands—we did so because we could no longer avoid the task of ruling Englishmen who for the purposes of trade had settled themselves on these shores. It was necessary that the natives should be protected from the greed of our own countrymen. It was necessary that our countrymen should be protected from each other, and it was also especially necessary to prohibit Englishmen from forming some abnormal community on the other side of the world which in after years we might be unable either to ignore or to acknowledge. Therefore we took New Zealand in hand, and so great were its natural advantages that, in spite of Maori wars—in spite even of the fact that up to this moment we are not masters of the Maoris—the new colony has become to us a source of honour and strength rather than a burden. With such an example before us we ought, perhaps, not to be afraid of Fiji; but the circumstances of Fiji are, I fear, much less promising than were those of New Zealand.

I have not visited Fiji, as I had hoped to do. In rambling about the world the months slip away so quickly that the traveller can rarely see all that he has intended to see; but I may be able to say something of the story of this new British possession which will let your readers know how it has come to pass that they have a part in the lordship over these distant islands. They were first discovered in 1643 by Tasman, the Dutchman, who, of all the adventurers in these seas, was certainly the greatest. From that time down to a period now just 40 years ago, they had no history which is interesting to us. They seem to have been originally peopled from the West by a race with crisp, black negro hair, such as were found in Australia, though probably more intelligent, and possessed of higher civilisation. To these had been added an influx from islands to the east of Fiji, from Tonga especially, of men with lank hair, the race which is general in the Polynesian islands, and hence there arose a people with divided habits, a double language, and causes for frequent war.

There are two large islands, Viti Levu and Vanua Levu, surrounded by over 200 smaller islands and islets. They lie exactly on the other side of the globe. The 180th line of longitude runs through them, which line is the same east or west from Greenwich. They are in the tropics, lying between the 16th and 19th lines south of the equator. It has been computed that the area of the islands together is equal to that of Wales. The population,[35] when we took possession of Fiji last

---

[35] There has been virtually no growth in the population of the islands.

year, was about 150,000. The scenery, especially on the eastern shores, is said to be very lovely. The heat is too severe for Europeans to work, as it is in very many parts of the British empire, but the islands are not subject to the malignity of any special disease, as are some of our West Indian possessions.

In 1835 a few white traders, Englishmen and Americans, probably mixed, first came to Fiji in quest of fortune, and established themselves in a place called Levuka, in one of the smaller islands. From that time to this, Levuka has been the white man's capital in Fiji; and two years later, missionaries settled themselves among the islands. Such have been the commencements of almost all modern colonisation. There has been the joint desire to make money and to proselytise—with the English as with the Spaniards. Now and again the love of freedom, and the desire to find new homes in which a man might say his prayers as he pleased, have driven wanderers forth and have created new countries; but the merchants and the missionaries have been the great discoverers of the world. It was they who by their joint action forced us to colonise New Zealand, and it is they who have now together compelled the Colonial Office to send a great governor to Fiji.

The name of Thakombau—here spelt as it is pronounced—will probably be familiar to most of your readers. He was born in 1804, and is still living, and in 1852 succeeded his father as chief of the largest of the Fijian tribes. But he was not then King of Fiji. A few years before the latter date there had appeared among the islands a stranger chief, a Tongan, named Maafu, who succeeded in establishing himself in the eastern or Windward Islands, as a rival to Thakombau. But it is with Thakombau that we English have chiefly dealt, and whose co-operation with Englishmen has caused Fiji to be this day an English colony. Two years after his father's death he became a Christian—as far as Christianity was possible to him—and renounced cannibalism. He and his wife were baptised, and he seems, at any rate, to have been convinced that there could be neither peace nor prosperity for his people unless they could be made secure, if not by British rule, at any rate by British protection. The other day, when the cession of the country was completed, he sent over, as a present to our Queen, his war-club, which had ever been to him the symbol of his authority. There is much in the character of the man which recommends itself to us, though he was a cannibal and a heathen, and though now, in his old age, his Christianity is not very intelligible to himself. He seems ever to have trusted the honesty and power of the British nation, and to have mingled with that trust a melancholy conviction that his own people could of themselves do nothing; and yet the Englishmen he had seen had not always been good specimens of their nationality. "Of one thing I am certain," he said to Sir Hercules Robinson, when they were negotiating the cession: "if we do not cede Fiji, the white stalkers on the beach, the cormorants, will open their mouths and swallow us." And again he said, "Fijians are of unstable character. A white man who wishes to get anything from a Fijian, if he does not succeed to-day, will try again to-morrow, till the Fijian is wearied out and gives in." He had learned that the weaker must give way to the stronger, and had perceived that it was better to abandon himself and his country at once to the justice of English rule than to be squeezed out of existence by the rapacity of individuals.

In the early days of chieftainship, various troubles came upon him. Maafu, his rival from Tonga, was strong against him, stirring up rebellion in the islands and separating the people. And then there were misfortunes with the Americans. In 1849 the house of the American consul was burned down, and compensation was claimed for that. In 1853, Levuka was burned, and, among other things, the houses and property of certain Americans were destroyed, for which further compensation was demanded. In 1855, an American officer came to assess this property, and demanded a payment of £9000 ($45,000). This seems to have been the beginning of Thakombau's pecuniary troubles. There was no means within his power of paying any such sum! If only England would take the islands and pay the money, things might at any rate be quiet! In 1858, the first offer of cession was made. Fiji should belong to England, if England would pay those hard American creditors. A deed of cession was sent to England in 1859, the British consul resident at Fiji taking it to London. The British residents in the islands were of course quite as anxious for the arrangement as Thakombau could be. But at that time the

British adult residents were only 166 in number, and in 1862 the offer was refused by us. The injury that 166 persons at the other side of the globe could do was not sufficient to induce us to accept the new burden.

Then, for twelve years, various struggles were made to carry on a native government on European plans and with European officers. In 1865, Thakombau, who had hitherto been only the first of the native chieftains, was elected president, and a constitution was formed similar to that which had been adopted under American auspices in the Sandwich Islands. At this time, Thakombau's chief minister was an American. But reliance on the United States did not last long, and in 1868 Thakombau was crowned king. There was, however, still that debt of £9000, and a clearly expressed determination on the part of the United States that the money must be forthcoming. As we know, our brethren in America are very urgent in the collection of such debts. Then a company was formed in Melbourne called the Polynesian Company, to whom a charter was given conferring vast rights, on condition that the £9000 should be paid. The company was to have a monopoly of banking, freedom from taxation, and 200,000 acres of land. The Americans got their money, and the Polynesian Company entered in upon a small fraction of their land.

In 1871,Thakombau, who had already been declared king, was proclaimed a constitutional sovereign, and a parliament, consisting of twenty-five members, was elected—a parliament consisting of white men. The first thing, of course—I believe I may say the only thing—the parliament did was to get into debt. Establishments and expenditure were sanctioned amounting to double the revenue which could be collected. The bickerings of the Europeans were incessant. Civil wars broke out among the natives, which had to be put down by a British man-of-war. Fresh offers of cession were made; and, in the meantime, King Thakombau was at his wit's ends, and the British fortune-hunters were in terrible lack of security for their ventures. Money was borrowed at almost whatever rate of interest might be demanded. The one thing wanted was government. Cotton could be grown, and sugar, and fortunes might be made, if only some real government were possible—some security that property would be protected by law. A Fijian parliament with poor King Thakombau at its head and self-appointed English ministers could do nothing but get into debt. Some strong staff on which the little place might lean with safety was necessary to its existence. If England would not take it, Fiji must become a mere nest of robbers, and a curse to that side of the world—especially a curse to our Australasian colonies, which are comparatively near to it.

The nest of robbers and the curse might have been endured by England, were it not that it would have been a British nest. The men who were practically declaring that they were willing enough to carry on their operations honestly, under the laws, if laws were provided for them, but that, lacking laws, they must live lawlessly, were Englishmen. No minister at home would send out a man-of-war and take every Briton out of Fiji. Thus the acceptance of the islands became a duty, and almost a necessity. After repeated offers we appointed two commissioners to inquire as to the terms of cession. The terms first offered were, of course, such as could not be accepted. Pensions were demanded. Money was demanded. Stipulations as to land were demanded. It was natural enough that King Thakombau should be instigated by his white ministers to ask for much, and that Englishmen living so far away from home should think that much might be got. A great power, taking on itself the burden of ruling these islands at the other side of the world, could submit to no bargaining. In July, 1874, our governor at New South Wales, Sir Hercules Robinson, was desired to go over to the islands and take possession of them, if the chiefs and men in authority there would unite in giving them up trustfully to British dominion. He arrived at Levuka on the 23rd of September, and on the 10th October, 1874, a deed of cession was executed at Levuka by all the chiefs, and by Sir Hercules, under which, without any terms, the islands were ceded to British rule.

How far our generosity may go in accepting the old Fijian pecuniary liabilities is perhaps not as yet decided—at any rate, is not absolutely known; but it is understood that we must begin our rule by lending Fiji about £150,000, of which £9000 will go to repay the company who settled those bitter American claims; and that we are setting on foot a government which will cost £30,000 a year, with the expectation of a revenue amounting to £20,000. The prospect is not a comfortable one to the British taxpayer, who will probably have no direct interest in Fiji; but the thing has been done before, and England has borne it, and, in spite of all our resolutions to the contrary, will probably be repeated.

An additional melancholy has been thrown over our entry upon this new possession by the breaking out of a frightful epidemic at the very moment. Some wretched vessel carried the measles into the islands; and out of a population of 250,000 souls, more than 50,000 have perished. Throughout the whole of Fiji, one in five has gone! Of course it is felt by these poor savages that death has come upon them as a penalty for their want of patriotism, and of course there are not wanting among them leaders who inculcate the idea. Such a mortality will appear to many as though the whole population were destroyed. Now, as I write, the destruction has passed away, and gradually the terrible feeling of which I have spoken will die out.

As soon as the transfer was completed, Thakombau, with some of his relatives and followers, paid a visit to Sir Hercules Robinson at Sydney, and was entertained in semi-regal state. The old man expressed himself pleased with everything, and was evidently gratified at the treatment he received. But he did not like the life. He has now gone back to his own land, and lives as a pensioner on the English Crown, with certain magisterial authority still in his hands. It is a singular termination to the career of one who has eaten his enemies, and who lived for sixty years as a heathen and a cannibal.

Letter XVIII

WHAT ARE WE to do with the South Sea Islands? It
might seem that this is a needless question, and that
we Englishmen as Englishmen are not required to do
anything with the South Sea Islands. At home, perhaps, as a people, we do not trouble ourselves much
about them. We are aware that there are many hundred
little specks of land lying about the Pacific Ocean,
chiefly within the tropics, inhabited by savage races,
many of them inhabited by cannibals, among whom
missionaries have gone from ourselves and other civilised people; but the islands do not belong to us. Why,
then, should it be a care to us to ask what is to be
done with them? And yet the question is constantly
getting itself asked, and is forcing an answer. Englishmen go and settle among them, and have to be looked
after. It cannot be permitted that English subjects,
gone half-wild with the license begotten by long absence, but still with enough of civilisation left for
ascendency over the absolute savage, should be allowed
to live as they please in these remote spots. And then
there is that great question of labour, with the attend-
ant question of slavery. Kidnapping cannot be allowed.
At any rate, let there be no British kidnapping. These
poor cannibals have thews and sinews, and if taken to
other lands can be made to work and become profitable. Let them go and work like other labourers if they

please; but they shall not be taken against their will. At any rate they shall not be taken by English ships or by English speculators. In this way there has grown up a most complicated question. The islands which we call Fiji have forced themselves upon us, and have become a British colony, from these causes. We are now being invited to undertake the difficult and very disagreeable task of annexing the enormous island called Papua, or New Guinea. And we maintain ships of war running about among the islands generally, trying to maintain justice, struggling to do some little good among these poor people; making an effort—alas, too often futile—to carry Christianity with them, at considerable expense, and sometimes with results to ourselves which are most disastrous. The missionary work, too, superadds itself so naturally to that which we must suppose to be more distinctly authorised by the Government at home. How is it possible for a humane and pious man moving about among these poor creatures not to attempt to endow them with the glorious gifts which he himself feels that he possesses? Thus attempts are made, and intercourse is established. Benevolent men, who would so fain be beneficent, go among them believing that kindness and justice will be understood and will prevail. But all who go are not kind, or even just. The rough, red-handed skipper, who has lived among these people till he has taught himself to regard them as no better than brute animals, is solely intent on making money out of them. In looking into the treatment which the South Sea Islanders have received from the white races, one finds the noblest conduct mixed with the most ignoble—self-devotion and pure philanthropy on one side, with greed and utter disregard for human suffering on the other. The poor savage, who certainly does not desire our good services, and who looks upon us at first as an intruder, whether we come for good or evil, cannot distinguish the God-like visitor from him who is simply fiendish; hence come mistakes, recriminations, punishments, and revenge, which have too often led to disasters so serious as to make us almost wish that no British ship might ever again be sent by Government to these islands. The late murder of Commodore Goodenough[36] at Santa Cruz was such a disaster.

But we know that we cannot cease our endeavours or get rid of duties in regard to stray British subjects because even such a man as Commodore Goodenough has been slain in the performance of his self-appointed task. And therefore it is that, as these troubles come upon us again and again, we have to ask ourselves what we mean to do with the South Sea Islands. There is too commonly a feeling in favour of annexation on the part of those who are concerned on the spot—either of entire annexation, with a thoroughly British government, or of partial annexation, with some ascendant British resident, who shall be practically supreme. It will always seem to a man that his own work is the really important thing that the world requires to have done. And when it becomes a man's work to defend these poor South Sea Islanders, he

---

[36] James Graham Goodenough (1830–1875), an extremely able and accomplished officer. He was wounded August 12 and died August 20, 1875.

soon teaches himself to feel that an English governor, with an English staff and an English man-of-war, would do it all, and turn almost hell into heaven. Let England call an island her own, let her fly her own flag there, and say that Victoria is Queen, and kidnapping may be stopped—not only kidnapping by Englishmen, but by Frenchmen also, and by Dutch. New Zealand was colonised for such reasons. But then New Zealand is not in the tropics.

I will tell very shortly the story of Commodore Goodenough. Commodore Goodenough was in command of the squadron employed in the Pacific, of which the headquarters are at Sydney. He had taken Sir Arthur Gordon, the new governor, to Fiji, and had afterwards gone on a cruise among the islands in her Majesty's ship Pearl. Lying in a curve running east and south-east from New Guinea are first the Solomon Islands, then the Santa Cruz group, and nearly south of them the New Hebrides. The inhabitants of all these are as yet but little known, are very savage, and are supposed to be cannibals. [On] one of these—at Vate, or Sandwich, among the New Hebrides—there is a settlement of white people, chiefly English or speakers of English, who grow a little cotton, and are probably concerned in the exportation of labour to New Caledonia. In the course of last year (1874) a small vessel from our squadron visited this place, with the direct object, no doubt, of repressing illegal traffic. Afterwards another vessel, the Sandfly, went up north among the Santa Cruz Islands, with the intention of getting general information about these islanders, and of doing any good that might be done to them. Where our men-of-war have gone, or any of the small craft which accompanies them, the object has never been, of late years, either lust of conquest or lust of gain. So much, I think, may be said with certainty. The idea has been to do some good if any good was possible. But this expedition of the Sandfly was not fortunate. Either the islanders did not understand us, or we did not understand them. They endeavoured to force their way on board. An arrow was fired, and they were repulsed. None of our men were hurt, and the Sandfly went away. On the 12th of August last, the month in which I am now writing, the commodore landed on the spot off which this misfortune had taken place. It was at Carlisle Bay, on the northern shore of the island Santa Cruz, in the Santa Cruz group. He says, in a letter written to his wife on that day, "I am going on shore to the spot where the Sandfly was attacked, to see if I cannot make friends with the unfortunates. They seem most friendly, and anxious to be civil, coming out to us in canoes, and looking as if they wished for peace." On the Tuesday following, going on with the same letter, he says, "But I was mistaken." It seems that he could not endure the idea that there should be among these islands any people who should have reason to think that he or any of those under him were their enemies. The philanthropy of the man was of so warm a nature that he could not bring himself to believe evil even of them. In discussing their condition with myself, when I have, I confess, expressed doubt as to their aptitude for lessons of a high

order, he has rebuked my hardness with a tenderness
which was peculiar to him—with a courtesy which I
think never could have forsaken him—and he has told
me that his experience taught him to think that they
were fit recipients for any good tidings which might be
brought to them. Well, on the 12th of August, in latitude about 10 south, longitude 166 east, he landed on
the beach near a little village containing eight or nine
huts, taking the solitary precaution of being himself
the first to jump out of the boat. He had with him his
secretary and five men, and was followed by a large
boat with eight or ten officers and a dozen men. He
had determined to go unarmed, but had allowed two
men in the second boat to carry pistols with them. As
he approached the shore he signalled to the ship that a
third boat should be sent with arms, and this was
done. He had probably observed that the natives
whom he saw clustering on the beach were not accompanied by their women and children, and, from his
knowledge of the habits of the people, had taken this
as betokening a want of amity. When he landed he
made presents to the savages, and the usual bartering
began—the exchange of cloth and hatchets for beads
and teeth, and what are generallly called "curios."
Then came a sharp shower of rain, and they were invited to take shelter under a shed and beneath the
trees, which came close down to the shore, almost
overhanging the water. Then he was invited to walk
on to a larger village, about a mile distant, and
started, accompanied by his secretary; but when he
had gone a short distance he seemed to fear the

separation between himself and his party, and returned. It is impossible to avoid feeling that he had determined to trust the islanders, with a conviction—though not quite a thorough conviction—that by doing so he might make them trustworthy, and that he had then remembered how great was his responsibility on behalf of others. He came back to the men whom he had left, and whom he had ordered not to leave the beach, and gave directions that they should go down to the boats. One or two were still bartering with natives, and in collecting them there was some little delay. When the commodore had turned for the last time—or, rather, as he was turning—he saw a savage raise his bow to his hip, and in that position let fly an arrow. This struck him on his side, and as he pulled it out he renewed his orders for the men to hurry down. Then there was a flight of arrows, most of them coming from natives hidden high in the branches among the trees. Five sailors were wounded besides the commodore, and by the return fire from our men two natives were shot, and probably killed. It seems that there were about 40 or 50 of these islanders collected, and that they were all armed with bows and arrows, with the exception of one man.

It was thought that the wounds received would hardly be serious unless the arrows were poisoned. While the men were in the boats the punctures were sucked, and when they had been on board for a day or two in the hands of the surgeons there was not at first much to fear. The question of course arose whether punishment should be exacted, and, if so, what punishment.

The commodore was inclined to leave them without any display of his power, remembering that the poor wretches were savages upon whom intrusion had been made, who could not know but that they had to deal with enemies who had come there to take away their young men and to steal their produce. Among those with him there was, of course, a first feeling to exact a bloody revenge for the treachery of the attack. Then he took a middle course, and ordered that the huts of the small village should be burned, giving special orders that neither a life should be taken nor a man hurt. A volley of blank cartridges was fired to frighten away the natives, and then a boat went ashore, and the huts were burned.

All this happened on a Thursday, and it was not till the next Tuesday that danger was feared. Then symptoms set in from which the doctors began to perceive that the arrows had probably been poisoned. Whether they were poisoned or not is still a question; but, as three of the six men wounded died of tetanus about the eighth or ninth day, it is probable that such was the case. Among the officers the commodore was wounded, and he was struck twice. Five sailors were struck, of whom two died, the other three regaining their health.

The conduct of the gallant leader of these men, when he was told that he was to die, was perhaps more interesting to those who were with him and to those who loved him than it can be made to your readers; but perhaps I may be permitted to say that it was of a piece with the life he had lived. He had himself carried on deck, and then spoke to his men such language as I do not dare to repeat here—words that were as beautiful as they were full of hope and contentment. And he sent messages of love to his wife and children, and gave directions how the sad tidings should be broken to her before her heart should have been elated by hearing that his ship was coming into harbour. On Friday, August 20, he died; and they brought him on shore, and we buried him with his two shipmates upon the hill, on the north shore, over Sydney harbour, in one of the loveliest spots ever formed by nature. She was there, the broken-hearted widow with her two children, the knowledge of whose loss was yet hardly more than twenty-four hours old—a sight never to be forgotten. And we all of us had to remember that in this futile attempt to make friends with the few natives of a little island, England had lost one of her best seamen—a man tender as he was brave, a man of science, full of the highest aspirations, fit for any great work—such a one as no nation can afford to lose lightly.

And now the question recurs with which I began this letter—what are we to do with the South Sea Islands? There will probably be a strong feeling at home that, because one of our great officers has been murdered in the execution of his duty, some vengeance should be taken; and yet can we fairly say that these islanders were to blame, acting as they did according to their lights? The island is theirs, and when we first went among them we exacted heavy retribution because they did not submit themselves to the overtures of peace which we were making to them. Probably there had been former visits under other flags—perhaps under our own—which had left behind them nothing but a sense of injury. It is certain that we do not mean to take possession of those lands for our own purposes—as we have done in Australia and New Zealand, in which, though our coming has exterminated, or will soon exterminate, the natives, even so sad a result as that is justified to our consciences by the opening of new homes to men of higher races. If we had all the islands lying within the tropics we could not find in them a fitting domicile for a single working European. If we look round the world within the tropics we must come to that conclusion as to the centre belt. And certainly we do not want an extended dominion over black subjects. The missionary tells us we may make Christians of them. I will not contradict the missionary, whose work is entitled to our loving respect. But I cannot but see that hitherto his success has hardly been sufficient to justify the assistance of our ships of war. At present it seems that we do not quite know what to do, and that we drift into the possession of undesirable so-called colonies. Perhaps the unfortunate loss which I have just recorded may lead to some fixed and definite policy in the matter.

Letter XIX

ON THE 28th August I left Sydney for this city, intending to call at Auckland, in New Zealand, and at Honolulu, the capital of the Sandwich Islands. For some
years past, various attempts have been made—not,
hitherto, with entire success—to establish a route for
mails and passengers from England to New South
Wales viâ New York and San Francisco, in opposition
to the eastern route by Suez; and in this attempt New
Zealand has been combined. New Zealand, no doubt,
will gain something, as that colony has never been
connected with the mother country by any direct
branch of the Peninsular and Oriental Steam[ship]
Company; but the desire on the part of New South
Wales has seemed to me to be irrational. The time, as
at present arranged, from London to Sydney by Brindisi and the Peninsular and Oriental steamers, is
forty-nine days; by New York and San Francisco it is
fifty days; and the experience of the last year or two
tends to show that time is more accurately kept by
the eastern route, viâ Suez, than by the way over the
American continent. For passengers the Peninsular
and Oriental route is, on the whole, considerably the
cheaper; for the carriage of her mails to San Francisco,
New South Wales now pays £45,000 per annum—a
sum considerably in excess of the amount she would
have to pay for the continuation of the services of the

Peninsular and Oriental steamers from Melbourne to Sydney. I am not aware of any reason for the choice the colony has made, other than the desire which the Australian colonies have to possess institutions independent one of another. From the nature of her position, Victoria must be served with her mails before New South Wales, if those mails are sent from England eastwards; therefore New South Wales likes to have a route of her own. The new contract under which the mail route across the Pacific is now about to be worked is, I think, the third which has been made within a few years, independently of the late temporary arrangement, which of all has been the most satisfactory. The new enterprise is altogether American, and has been undertaken by the North Pacific Steam[ship] Company, which runs steamers from San Francisco to China and Japan. Whether it will be more successful than its predecessors I will not attempt to prophesy. The barrier to success, no doubt, lies in the difficulty of obtaining freight. California sends nothing to Australia which will pay for steam carriage, nor does she import anything from Australia of that nature. Coal from New South Wales does find its way to California, and wheat from California to New South Wales, but neither one nor the other will endure the cost of steam conveyance for 30 days.

My sojourn in New Zealand on the present occasion was but for 24 hours, and I am not, therefore, prepared to say much that is new from personal observation; but having visited the colony before, and been at some trouble to learn the nature of its institutions and to weigh its chances of prosperity, I was glad to avail myself even of that short time to make inquiry as to its doings. I had heard that there were two subjects of present paramount interest in the colony—the abolition of provincial governments, and the financial arrangements of Sir Julius Vogel.[37] Some of your readers may probably be unaware—most Englishmen, probably, are unaware—that New Zealand, in imitation of the United States, has established within her borders eight subordinate provincial or state governments. These are called Otago, Canterbury, Nelson, Marlborough, Wellington, Hawksbay, Taranaki, and Auckland. Each of these has a little parliament of its own, independent of the central parliament at Wellington. They collect and spend taxes, they manage the affairs of the state, and gentlemen composing them are paid for their services. When it is remembered that the total present population of the colony is about 325,000[38]—equal to that of a single first-class provincial town at home—it will hardly be thought that there is room for eight parliaments, besides the central parliament—each with its own Speaker, its own records, its own government and opposition sides, and each with its own expenses; and there will be found room for fear that gentlemen with leisure, means, and capacity for the work will hardly be found in sufficient number among so small a community. That has at any rate become the opinion of the majority of the

[37] Sir Julius Vogel (1835–1899), premier of New Zealand, was a shrewd, if somewhat rash, administrator. His ambitious spend-lend program might have succeeded had not a steady decline in wool and grain prices brought on a fifteen-year depression.

[38] In 1926—1,344,469.

central parliament of the colony, which has, as a matter of course, in conjunction with the governor, the power of abolishing all these inferior representative assemblies. But, though there is a great majority in favour of such abolition, there is a strong opposing minority, whose chief strength lies in the voices of the superintendents or governors of the provinces themselves. These superintendents—for such is their name, though their position has been intended to be analogous with that of the state governors in the United States—will themselves be abolished by the new measure; and as a seat in the central parliament is compatible with their position, and as they are almost invariably elected so to sit, they are enabled to lift up their voices loudly in their own protection. When I was there they were doing so, and were threatening to overcome the proposed reform by talking on to the end of the session. And it must be owned that they had a strong constitutional ground on which to base their reasoning. So radical a change in the nature of the government of the country would amount, no doubt, to an alteration in the existing constitution; and these gentlemen assert that no such alteration should be made without an appeal to the country at large. They maintain that the present Assembly should be dissolved, and that new elections should be made in reference to this special matter, so that each elector may have an opportunity of recording his vote either for a provincialist or a non-provincialist. In this the minority is probably right. But I believe that the colony at large is undoubtedly in favour of abandoning its petty parliaments, and that they will be abandoned.

Sir Julius Vogel and his loans is perhaps a more important matter. If anything can ruin a young colony, one would say such a debt as eighteen millions sterling would ruin a colony possessing a population no higher than 325,000; and such, under the successful arrangements lately made by Sir Julius, is now the debt of New Zealand. This, I think, imposes an individual debt of about £56 upon every colonist, man, woman, and child, with an annual burden of about £2 3s. each for interest. We are apt to think that we bear a very crushing debt at home, when the interest defrayed by every man, woman, and child is about 17s. 6d. each. In England, too, efforts have been made to remove taxation as much as possible from the poor and throw it upon the rich; whereas no such efforts can be made in a colony which has no rich class and no poor class. If an average working-man's family may be supposed to consist of four persons, then the average working man will have to contribute 3s. 3d. a week, or nearly a day's wages per week, towards the interest on the public debt. I do not know of any conditions of national indebtedness so high as this. And it seems to be understood in New Zealand that if Sir Julius Vogel remains in power the system of borrowing, of which he is so great a master, is to be continued. According to his theory, the outlay of money which a government is thus enabled to make will produce an amount of prosperity which the debt cannot injuriously affect. The outlay, no doubt, is made, and pleasant results are the immediate consequence. One pleasant result is the popularity of the politician who has dared to cast high wages broadcast through the land, and who, as a natural consequence of such liberality, will receive the suffrages of those who have for a while lived and thriven on his system. Such a system may last the time, and may answer the purposes, of this or that bold and speculative politician; but, with a country as with an individual, the time will come when debts must be paid or bankruptcy ensue. I do not predict bankruptcy to New Zealand. The mother country would probably save so well-loved a colony from that position. But if she did so, she would demand to have the management of its finances for a time in her own hands. It seems to me to be quite possible that Sir Julius Vogel, if he remain long enough in power, may bring New Zealand to this condition.

From New Zealand the run across the tropics, north by east, to the Sandwich Islands, is one of thirteen or fourteen days. We had no extreme heat, the thermometer never rising above 83 or 84. No doubt the route by the Red Sea and Ceylon is, in this respect, more oppressive than that across the Pacific. I slept on deck the whole way, but I was the only passenger who felt disposed to make this escape from the cabins. Since the British mails have been carried across the American continent, the steamers on their way to New Zealand have always called at Honolulu, thereby bringing that place and the Sandwich Islands generally within the limits of the civilised world. But under the new contract Honolulu is not included. The steamers are bound to go from San Francisco to the Fiji Islands, and from thence will branch, one to Sydney, in New South Wales, and the other to Auckland, in New Zealand, from whence it will run down the New Zealand coast to Dunedin. If this programme be carried out strictly, the Sandwich Islands will be left out very much in the cold. But as there is always freight to be had between [San] Francisco and the islands, both ways, I think the company will endeavour to make the slight detour necessary for the call.

The Sandwich Islands form another of those lands as to the destiny of which the world at large, and especially the English world, is so much in doubt. In the course of these letters I have spoken of Papua or Borneo, of the Fiji Islands, and the Santa Cruz Islands, and have referred to the difficulty, or perhaps impossibility, of connecting the native races of these regions with European or American civilisation. The question in regard to the Sandwich Islands is the same—although in the Sandwich Islands the progress already made is much greater than that achieved in any of the South Sea Islands, unless we include New Zealand. In New Zealand civilisation has been established, but it has been established for the benefit of Europeans, and has been based, in fact, on the extermination of the native races. The Maoris are going fast, and are in fact nearly gone. The Fiji Islands have been annexed to our dominion, and the Fijians will go. New Zealand is not tropical, and will therefore be the permanent home of an English-speaking, working community. The Fiji Islands are tropical, and will therefore never reach this condition. The Sandwich Islands are also tropical, and will never afford the means of living to any race that has sprung from European parents. But, from the circumstances of its position—and partly from the nature of its inhabitants, who, though but little prone to work, are more prone than other islanders who live nearer to the line—this spot in the Pacific Ocean has acquired a certain amount of hybrid prosperity, which is almost absurd in its details and which certainly cannot endure.[39] In 1866 the islands contained 58,765 native inhabitants, and in 1872, 51,531. The fact of this diminution is of itself sufficient to show that contact with white people is producing its usual effect among these races—that, namely, of extermination. In 1866 there were 4194 aliens, including Chinese; and in 1872 there were 5366. The chief produce of the islands is sugar. The lesson, therefore, to be read, is that the region will become the property of American or English sugar-growers, and the work on the plantations will be done by Chinese or coolie immigrants, a result very much opposed to the theory of those who have wished to build up an Hawaiian monarchy.

The Sandwich Islands were so named by Captain Cook after Lord Sandwich, who was his friend and patron, and was also at the head of the Admiralty Board. Captain Cook first visited them in 1778, and again in 1779, when he was murdered there—as is generally said—while endeavouring to recover a boat

[39] Trollope would have thought it incredible that fifty years later the city of Honolulu alone should have had twice the population he cites for the entire islands.

which had been taken by the natives. A question may be fairly raised as to the justness of the accusation conveyed by the term. A difference of opinion as to Captain Cook's right to dominion seems to have arisen. No doubt it was necessary that Captain Cook, in the pursuance of his objects, should domineer. A white man, when he finds himself among savages, is bound at any rate to endeavour to be the master. Contests and quarrels will arise. When the white man, at the cost of a certain amount of blood, achieves his object—as he generally does—we are sorry that he has been found to kill one or perhaps a dozen natives. But when the invaded savage succeeds in slaughtering a Briton, that Briton has always been murdered. Captain Cook was a great and good man, and a most valuable British subject; but I do not feel myself called upon to execrate the homicidal tendency of the Hawaiian who killed him with a dagger in a free fight. Before that time the inhabitants of Hawaii, as the islands were then called, had been cannibals; but it seems that they had dropped the custom before Cook's coming.

In those days there was, and ever since there has been, a royal family in the islands. The rule exercised by the old kings seems to have been in the main despotic. In latter years, especially since the finding of gold in California—from the coast of which the Sandwich Islands are but 800 miles distant[40]—Americans and Englishmen have flocked in, and have between them obtained practical possession of the capital,

---

[40] An error. Actually the distance is 2604 miles.

Honolulu. Honolulu is unlike, and is very superior to, any other town on the world's surface which at the present moment is nominally under the dominion of savages. There is an excellent hotel, with prices of a highly civilised amount. Gas is made there. Balls and dinner parties are given. And you may have any number of clothes washed by a steam apparatus in half a dozen hours. When you inquire who provides and protects all these good things, you learn that you are living under a limited monarchy, the monarch of the day being King Kalakaua, who is the descendant of a race of kings who rejoiced in the name of Ka-meha-meha. This king is assisted by a parliament, of which the upper house consists of twenty nobles named by himself. These nobles may be natives or foreigners. There are natives among the members, and there are also Americans and Englishmen. There is also a house of twenty-eight representatives elected biennially, which meets every two years, and is also of a mixed character. The king has a cabinet, in which I think I may say that the American element predominates. There is a chief justice, who is an American, and two other judges—I believe of the same nation. It need hardly be said that in this way the Americans and English between them have invented a form of government under which they may be ruled according to their own wishes without the exercise of any nominal protectorate. The arrangement is one similar to that proposed for the judges in our new colony at Fiji. There shall be an English judge and a native judge. The English judge may sit alone, but not the native judge. When they agree, the decision will of course stand; but should they disagree, the decision of the English judge shall be the decision of the court.

Good purposes may perhaps be achieved by this playing at the conversion of savages to civilisation. Good purposes have been achieved at Honolulu, the place having become safe for the investment of capital. But it is well, I think, that we should know what has been achieved, and also what has not and cannot be done.

Letter XX

MY WAY HOME from the Sandwich Islands to London took me to San Francisco, across the American continent and [to] New York, whence I am now writing to you my last letter of this series. I had made this journey before, but had on that occasion reached California too late to visit the now world-famous valley of the Yo Semite, and the big pine trees which we call Wellingtonias. On this occasion I made the excursion, and will presently tell the story of the trip; but I must first say a few words as to the town of San Francisco.

I do not know that in all my travels I ever visited a city less interesting to the normal tourist, who, as a rule, does not care to investigate the ways of trade, or to employ himself in ascertaining how the people around him earn their bread. There is almost nothing to see in San Francisco that is worth seeing. There is a new park in which you may drive for six or seven miles on a well-made road, and which, as a park for the use of the city, will, when completed, have many excellences. There is also there the biggest hotel in the world—so the people of San Francisco say—which has cost a million sterling—five millions of dollars—and is intended to swallow up all the other hotels. It was just finished, but not opened, when I was there. There is an inferior menagerie of wild beasts, and a place called the Cliff House, to which strangers are taken to hear seals bark. Everything, except hotel prices, is dearer here than at any other large town I know, and the ordinary traveller has no peace left him, either in public or private, by touters who wish to persuade him to take this or the other railway route into the Eastern States. There is always a perfectly cloudless sky overhead, unless when rain is falling in torrents, and perhaps nowhere in the world is there a more sudden change from heat to cold on the same day. I think I may say that strangers will generally desire to get out of San Francisco as quickly as they can, unless, indeed, circumstances may have enabled them to enjoy the hospitality of the place. There is little or nothing to see, and life at the hotels is not comfortable. But the trade of the place, and the way in which money is won and lost, are alike marvellous. I found 10s. a-day to be about the lowest rate of wages paid to a man for any kind of work in the city; and the average wages of a housemaid—who is, of course, found in everything but her clothes—to be over £70 per annum. All payments in California are made in coin, whereas in the other States of the Union except California, Oregon, and Nevada, moneys are paid in depreciated notes, so that the two dollars and a-half per day which the labourer earns in San Francisco are as good as three and a quarter in New York. No doubt this high rate of pay is met by an equivalent in the high cost of many articles, such as clothing and rent; but it does not affect the price of food, which to the labouring man is the one important item of expenditure. Consequently, the labouring man in California has a position which I have not known him to achieve elsewhere.

In trade there is a speculative rashness which ought to ensure ruin, according to our old-world ideas, but seems to be rewarded by very general success. The stranger may of course remember, if he pleases, that the millionaire who builds a mighty palace is seen and heard of and encountered at all corners, while the bankrupt will probably sink unseen into obscurity. But in San Francisco there is not much of bankruptcy, and, when it does occur, no one seems to be so little injured as the bankrupt. There is a good nature, a forbearance, and an easy giving of trust, which to an old-fashioned Englishman like myself seems to be most dangerous, but which I was assured there forms the readiest mode of building up a great commercial community.The great commercial community is there, and I am not prepared to deny that is has been built after that fashion. If a young man there can make friends, and can establish a character for honesty to his friends and for smartness to the outside world, he can borrow almost any amount of money without security, for the purpose of establishing himself in business. The lender, if he feel sure that he will not be robbed by his protégé, is willing to run the risk of unsuccessful speculation.

As we steamed into the Golden Horn[41] the news reached us that about a month previously the leading bank in San Francisco, the Bank of California, had "burst up" for some enormous amount of dollars, and

---

[41] A slip of the traveler's pen for Golden Gate.

that the manager, who was well known as one of the richest men and as perhaps the boldest speculator in the state, had been drowned the day following.[42] But we also heard that payments would be resumed in a few days—and payments were resumed before I left the city; that no one but the shareholders would lose a dollar, and that the shareholders were ready to go on with any amount of new capital; and that not a single bankruptcy in the whole community had been caused by the stoppage of the bank, which had been extended for a period over a month! How came it to pass, I asked, of course, that the collapse of so great a monetary enterprise as the Bank of California should pass on without a general panic, at any rate in the city? Then I was assured that all those concerned were good-natured, that everybody gave time, that bills were renewed all round, and that in an hour or two it was understood that no one in San Francisco was to be asked for money just at that crisis. To me all this seemed to be wrong. I have always imagined that severity to bankrupt debtors—that amount of severity which requires that a bankrupt shall really be a bankrupt—is the best and indeed the only way of ensuring regularity in commerce, and of preventing men from tossing up with other people's money in the confidence that they may win and cannot lose. But such doctrines are altogether out of date in California. The money of depositors was scattered broadcast through the mining speculations of the district, and no one was a

---

[42] The failure of the Bank of California, to which Trollope refers, occurred August 25. See John P. Young, *San Francisco* (San Francisco, 1912), II, 504–508.

bit the worse for it except the unfortunate gentleman who had been, perhaps happily, removed from a community which had trusted him long with implicit confidence, and which still believed him to be an honest man, but which would hardly have known how to treat him had he survived. To add to the romance of the story it should be said that, though this gentleman was drowned while bathing, it seems to be certain that his death was accidental. It is stated that he was struck with apoplexy while in the water.

I was taken to visit the Stockbrokers' Board in San Francisco—that is, the room in which mining shares are bought and sold. The reader should understand that in California, and, still more, in the neighbouring State of Nevada, gold mining and silver mining are now very lively. The stock-jobbing created by these mines is carried on in San Francisco, and is a business as universally popular as was the buying and selling of railway shares during our railway mania. Everybody is at it. The housemaid of whom I have spoken as earning £70 per annum buys Consolidated Virginia or Ophir stock with that money; or perhaps she prefers Chollar Potosi, or Best and Belcher, or Yellow Jacket, or Buckeye. She probably consults some gentleman of her acquaintance, and no doubt in 19 cases out of 20 loses her money. But it is the thing to do, and she enjoys that charm which is the delectation of all gamblers. Of course, in such a condition of things there are men who know how the wind is going to blow, who make the wind blow this way or that, who can raise the price of shares by fictitious purchases and then sell, or depreciate them by fictitious sales and then buy. The housemaids and others go to the wall, while the knowing men build palaces, and seem to be troubled by no seared consciences. In the meantime the brokers drive a roaring trade—whether they purchase legitimately for others, or speculate on their own account. The Stock Exchange in London is, I believe, closed to strangers. The Bourse in Paris is open to the world, and at a certain hour affords a scene to those who choose to go and look at it of wild noise, unintelligible action, and sometimes apparently of demoniac fury. The uninitiated are unable to comprehend that the roaring herd in the pen beneath them are doing business. The Stock Exchange Board in San Francisco is not open to strangers as it is in Paris, but may be visited with an order, and by the kindness of a friend I was admitted. Paris is more than six times as large as San Francisco; but the fury at San Francisco is even more demoniac than in Paris. I thought that the gentlemen employed were going to hit each other between the eyes, and that the apparent quarrels which I saw already demanded the interference of the police. But the uproarious throng were always obedient, after slight delays, to the ringing hammer of the chairman, and as each five minutes' period of internecine combat was brought to an end I found that a vast number of mining shares had been bought and sold. Perhaps a visit to this chamber when the stockbrokers are at work, between the hours of eleven and twelve, is, of all sights in San Francisco, the one best worth seeing.

A visit to the Yo Semite Valley from San Francisco

requires a long and very tedious journey. The tourist first travels by railway from the city to Merced, about 140 miles, the first 100 of which are on the line which runs across the continent. At Merced he sleeps, finding there a very comfortable American hotel, at which, however, they will refuse to clean his boots. On the following morning he will start at six by a four-horse stage-coach, which, travelling at the rate of five miles an hour, will bring him to the end of his first day's journey at six in the evening. Here he will be accommodated at a ranche or farm-house, which has gradually grown to be an inn, and will be treated with smiling, good-natured courtesy. The next day's coaching will take him into the valley, and on his way he will have passed through a grove of the immense pine trees which first gave celebrity to these regions.

The latter portion of this journey is made through a picturesque country, with fine hills and handsome timber, but it is not comparable in beauty to very many roads of a similar nature in Europe. The first part of the road—from Merced, through Snelling, and as far as Coulterville—is altogether interesting. I travelled over it in September, when the dust was almost unbearable. The beds of the river were almost dry; the greenswards had become yellow, and the midday heat was extreme. I can easily believe that in May and June it bears a very different aspect. But in May and June the visitors who unfortunately belong to the unprivileged sex can seldom be accommodated with beds. The dormitories in the hotels are devoted to ladies, while the gentlemen repose either under or upon the dinner tables. The crowd is apt to be so great that, when the meals are spread, enormous energy is required, or at least is often used, by those who are anxious to secure their meals. We had no grass and no water in the streams, but we had every attention shown to us at Mr. Black's hotel, at which we were the only guests.

Sightseeing in the valley has to be done on horse-back, and the horses provided for our use were very good. You would not give me space were I to attempt to convert your columns into a guide book for the Yo Semite. I may perhaps best use the few words which are at my command by saying that the chief glory of the place depends on the almost perpendicular steepness and on the enormous altitude of the rocks which hem it in. The Clouds Nest[43] rises to a height of 6450 feet above the valley, and the rock called Le Capitaine,[44] which to the naked eye seems to hang over if it be not perpendicular, is 3000 feet high. The highest summits of the valley are about 12,000 feet above the sea. The highest mountains of Europe are of course higher than any that there are here; but I know of no rocks in Europe or elsewhere which are to be compared to them. Early in the morning, just as the sun is rising, and again for perhaps an hour before it has set, the colours are beautiful and the effects magnificent. But during the close of the day everything is painfully white. It is not the whiteness of snow or of marble, but rather that of plaster of Paris. The substance which produces this effect is in fact granite.

---

[43] *I.e.*, Clouds' Rest. [44] *I.e.*, El Capitan.

The shapes of the summits are graceful and bold, but the mountains do not run into sharp peaks and serrated edges. Two of the most conspicuous are called the North and South Domes. The grandeur of the scene—and it is very grand—arises chiefly from the manner in which the precipitous sides of the mountains have been cut sheer down into the valley. In the spring and early summer the waterfalls must be very beautiful. They were beautiful when I was there, though from the scantiness of the mountain streams they were shorn of their great glory.

The return from the valley was exactly the same as the journey to it—hot, tedious, long, and dusty. Both going and coming I measured some of the big trees, finding the girth of the largest which I saw to be 78 feet. From the irregularity of the ground and the knobby excrescences which add to the size of the trees, accurate measurement is impossible, but I feel sure that I have rather understated than overstated the amount. The height of the highest trees yet discovered in California is by no means equal to that of some that have been found in Australia. I do not think that any tree exceeding 400 feet in height has been found in America, but a tree has been measured in Victoria which, when standing, exceeded 500 feet.

The traveller about to proceed from San Francisco to the East may accomplish a part of the journey to Yo Semite on his way. On returning he will stop at Latrop[45] and pick up the railway cars for New York, or whatever place may be his destination, thus saving

---

[45] *I.e.*, Lathrop.

the run of 100 miles back to San Francisco. As to my-self, business required me to return to the city, and I thus had the opportunity of making the unbroken journey from the Pacific to the Atlantic.

So many accounts have already been given of this journey that I need hardly detain your readers by describing it at length. It occupies seven days and seven nights, the start from San Francisco being made at eight a.m. During this time the traveller is continually travelling, except for the three spaces of twenty minutes each per diem which are allowed for eating. The undertaking seems to be, if not dangerous on account of fatigue, at any rate liable to great tedium and very much discomfort. I can only say that I never made a journey with less fatigue, less tedium, or less discomfort. I was peculiarly happy in my fellow-travellers; but as I have crossed twice and was thus lucky on both occasions, meeting people in the carriages whom I had never seen before and from whom I parted as old friends, I may presume that such is the usual condition of things. The traveller should, I think, trouble himself with the carriage of no eatables, as those supplied on the road are in every way sufficient. If he wishes the solace of wine or spirits he should take them with him. He will find himself provided with an excellent bed and with ample accommodation for washing his hands and face. The need of a bath at the end of the journey is certainly much felt.